A SEARCH
for
CIVILIZATION

JOHN NEF

Chairman
Committee on Social Thought
and Center of International Understanding
University of Chicago

GREENWOOD PRESS, PUBLISHERS
WESTPORT, CONNECTICUT

Library of Congress Cataloging in Publication Data

Nef, John Ulric, 1899-
    A search for civilization.

    Reprint of the 1962 ed. published by Regnery, Chicago.
    1. Civilization--Philosophy. I. Title.
[CB19.N42 1975]   909   75-1114
ISBN 0-8371-7987-4

Originally published in 1962 by Henry Regnery Company,
Chicago

Reprinted with the permission of Henry Regnery Company

Reprinted in 1975 by Greenwood Press,
a division of Williamhouse-Regency Inc.

Library of Congress Catalog Card Number 75-1114

ISBN 0-8371-7987-4

Printed in the United States of America

CB
19
N42
1975

To Nan

Contents

Preface

IT IS ONE of the great misfortunes of our era that, as men and women everywhere become increasingly interdependent, their training and their occupations become increasingly concerned with special subjects and special interests. The universal is more and more forgotten in the particular at a time when human survival is coming to depend as never before upon the common humanity of those who make the irrevocable decisions. With greater happiness than was ever before possible within our grasp, this misfortune may lead to total tragedy unless we can pluck the universal out of the particular in ways that will give it a concrete reality which it has lacked, and so, while retaining the richness of diversity, relate each particular to a universal purpose in which all men and women can share. Such a purpose could change men's thought, could help them to discover within them richer selves, so that they could find outlets for their energies in peace and construction never before open to them.

An old world is going out. *A Search for Civilization* is published in the hope it may help us to find a better one, that it may show there is an alternative to the total tragedy—the extinction of our race—which no lover of life can contemplate. And why is each of us born if not in love of life, in desire for lasting fulfillment of the life we have been given? I am told it was President Eisenhower who, in a flash of insight, observed that "there is no longer an alternative to peace." The great task before statesmen is not repeatedly to stand on the brink of war, but to edge closer to peace. How can we help them, and so help our fellow men and women?

I write of these overwhelmingly important matters as a man whose profession has been that of a practicing historian. From the beginning of my career as student, as writer and teacher, I have been ill at ease under the pressures that drive men and women to break their lives up into separate compartments, and, with their lives, their engagement in events and in other people: those they know and the rapidly growing numbers with whom they participate without realizing how or why or to what extent. As time has gone on, my uneasiness has been increased by a deepening conviction that all parts of an individual's life, together with all the important issues which he faces in a particular vocation and society, are organically interrelated. Now more than ever it is the nature and meaning of these interrelations, the connections between the particular and the universal, between each of the billions of living individuals and God, which excite my interest.

The concrete takes on reality only when its wider meaning is recognized and conveyed in terms of individual experiences. More often than not specialization, and what is regarded by scholars as a scientific approach to a particular subject, obscure such a meaning. Specialization has been accompanied by a growing emphasis on categories. Together these tendencies dehumanize the work that scholars present verbally or in writing.

When I began my special studies I already felt these limitations of growing specialization for any audience. In doing minute research amid the smell of old paper in European archives, in compiling statistics of coal shipments received at London during the reigns of the first Queen Elizabeth and the Stuarts, I found myself continually touched by a belief that, without the heart and the imagination, the mind can easily become a dogmatic, dreary and even sterile instrument for living or reliving any experience in which men and women are the actors. And can anyone make history live except by reliving it as far as this is possible, which means recreating as perfectly as he can the characters he encounters in old documents, or sees through the maze of statistics which the concern with quantitative knowledge of historical data has provided?

The fate of Americans is now indissolubly linked with that of all the other peoples who have inherited the earth. That is why we, in company with men and women of other countries and continents, must look beyond the particular states to which we belong. Such an outlook is extremely difficult to achieve. It depends on getting out of ourselves. One way of doing that, one way of working towards a human philosophy, is to saturate oneself with the language and the traditions of a society other than one's own, to the point of sharing something of its being, even of its essence. Why do I say one, instead of many other languages and societies?

It is somewhat as with marriage. The way to lose oneself is in one other person. An effort to commit oneself at the same time to many others may occupy one's time effectively, but it throws one back almost entirely on oneself for reference. At any rate I have found it to be so.

As a result of assignments as a professor in France, I have gained some experience in conversing, lecturing and writing in French. While my knowledge of France, her language and her people is most imperfect, I have had at least the advantage, which helps so much in groping towards a more comprehensive and just world view, of losing myself in a country different from the one in which I was born. This has led me to feel that it is through the richness of diversity that one gets a sense of the unity of the human race.

I was in Paris, on a voyage of discovery, at the time of the moving events which brought General de Gaulle to power and changed the form of republican government in his country. I was there for the purpose of founding, with the support of the administration and trustees of the University of Chicago, a *Center of International Understanding*. As I had already published two books in French, and as the persons who joined me then in the effort to form such a center were all French-speaking, my choice of their language for my new book was not unnatural. But I soon found I wanted to say the things I had to say to everyone, not only to those who understand French, and therefore I wanted to say them in every language my tongue could command. Alas there was only one other language I had even partly mastered—my own.

So I rethought this essay in English. A literal is always a treacherous translation. The Italians incorporated those words in a proverb, and nowhere does its truth appear plainer than when one is confronted, as I have been, with the task of converting what one wrote in a foreign language into one's own. The ideas and purposes which I had in mind when I began to write in French are still with me. But by taking to the English tongue I have embodied them in a fresh idiom partly because I was myself (at least so I hope) in the process of evolving.

Among the French friends who gave me, before and during the weeks when the Fifth Republic was born, generous moral and spiritual support in my effort to start a *Center of International Understanding,* two have since died. I think of them with particular gratitude. One was Jean Désy, formerly Canadian ambassador to France. By his criticism of the French text of my essay he helped me to develop my ideas in English, as well as to write less imperfectly than I should have otherwise in his language. The other was a much older friend, André Siegfried. He was the most vigorous animator of our project in April and early May 1958, just before the Algerian revolt of May 13. Without his enthusiasm for the Center, the group to which I now belong could hardly have come into existence. It is my responsibility to try to build on the foundation we laid together. This I can do only with the help of those other French friends who gave the project their support at the outset: Jacques Maritain, Jean Sarrailh, formerly rector of the University of Paris, Jacques de Bourbon Busset and Charles Morazé.

Every bit of this book, in both French and English, has been composed since I met the person to whom it is dedicated. If I had not met her, I should not have written it.

JOHN NEF

September 1961

A SEARCH FOR CIVILIZATION

PART I: WISDOM

CHAPTER I

The Foundation of Civilization

THE MATERIAL WORLD in which we now work, travel, amuse ourselves, create and fight is completely different from any known to history. "Industrial revolution" is a new phrase, apparently introduced into language only at the beginning of the nineteenth century.* A recent student of technological history plausibly maintains that there have been two industrial revolutions since the seventeen-eighties, and that the world is now in the throes of a third. All this has happened within the very short span of time the United States has been an independent nation. According to the criteria of this same authority, one can scan the whole historical process without finding another period of comparably decisive material change unless it was at the dawn of history, which archeologists have now pushed back many thousands of

---

* Nef, "The Industrial Revolution Reconsidered," in *War and Human Progress*, Cambridge, Mass., 1950, chap. xv.

years. Neither the Egyptians, the Persians nor the ancient Chinese, neither the Hellenes, the Romans nor the Moslems, ever participated in an "industrial revolution."

No wonder, then, that the historian is arrested by the suddenness with which new material conditions have appeared—the unprecedentedly rapid growth in population and in the volume of standardized, mechanically or automatically produced goods, the unprecedentedly rapid increase in the speed of movement. As far back as 1909, in a paper called "The Rule of Phase Applied to History," Henry Adams remarked on the fantastically rapid speeding up in the rate of change. "The acceleration of the comet," he wrote, "is much slower than that of society. The world did not double or treble its movement between 1800 and 1900, but, measured by any standard known to science . . . the tension and vibration and volume and so-called progression of society were fully a thousand times greater in 1900 than in 1800, the speed, when measured by electrical standards as in telegraphy, approached infinity, and had annihilated both space and time."*

The speed of change has hardly slackened since Adams wrote those words. In respect at least to travel through space, it has increased overwhelmingly; here the recent acceleration of history is without any precedent before 1909. The air age, foreseen in the seventeenth century by the Anglican Bishop Wilkins, has come upon us in the short span of fifty years. It is no longer merely sounds but human beings who are hurled about in the annihila-

* Henry Adams, *The Degradation of the Democratic Dogma*, New York, 1913, p. 303.

tion of space and time. We look back on the generation of Adams as conforming to a quiet place of living and vacationing as well as vocationing. That pace is now demoded, almost forgotten. It is revived only by curiosity seekers bound for historical adventure, who set to sea in sailboats built to simulate Christopher Columbus' caravelles, a name which, somewhat incongruously, has been given recently to ships that shoot through the air ten miles a minute.

Dazzled by the changes, men and women everywhere are impressed mainly by the sensational and the spectacular. But the penetration of outer space, the tracing of a route to the moon, the mass sensationalism of many television and radio programs and newspaper stories, do not seem to help with the vital problems of individual human relations. And it is upon the improvement of these that the possibility of dealing constructively with economic, social and political issues depends. The great problem facing human beings everywhere is how, in the throes of such unprecedented upheavals as these of recent times, people might come to live together on something approaching terms of decent friendship. The future of mankind is bound up with the creation of a reasonably harmonious world society, such as has never existed. Could it possibly be achieved?

It is difficult to believe it could unless common ideals and hopes, more tender than any that have predominated in the past, emerge out of the prevailing chaos of innumerable tongues, numerous and often conflicting religious teachings, extremes of material riches and poverty, different traditions and manners. The common

3

ideals and hopes, which are fundamental if mankind is to attain a measure of unity, are not to be obtained by making people all alike. One of the major obstacles to community is the stereotyped, mechanized lives that, under industrialism, men and women everywhere feel forced to live. Only great diversity of experience, and the richness such diversity can bring, the opportunities it can offer for comparisons in the light of good purposes, can provide the spiritual nourishment that is essential if people everywhere are to live a more civilized existence than has hitherto prevailed in even a small part of the planet.

What ends could men and women everywhere strive after with something approaching a common sense of ultimate purpose to bind them to one another, without losing the identity that alone gives value to personal relationships? Since the War of 1939-45 and the struggle for ascendency that has followed among the great powers—especially between communist Russia and the United States—the impression has spread that there are only two kinds of government capable of holding modern societies together. One is some form of totalitarianism, under which the final authority depends on a despot. The other is some kind of constitutionalism, where that authority is vested in representative assemblies and executive administrations, both chosen by universal suffrage, and in judiciaries which are supposed to be free from political, economic and social pressure.

The distinction is important, above all in so far as it reflects a deeper and more fundamental division of the principles that guide individuals in their lives. But, in

4

itself, it is only a political distinction, and therefore one between means rather than between ends. If it be treated as a matter of ultimate purpose, the distinction deteriorates into one of strategy devoid of principles; masses of people are pitted against other masses without issues worthy of defense.

If politics, along with education and economic organization, is to serve man, people must acquire deeper, more concrete knowledge of what this creature is that they want to help. Why are men and women put on earth? Can one conceive of happiness, as the philosophers often have, as their final purpose? And what meaning should be attached to the word happiness?

Such questions can, and they ought to, introduce us to a rich and varied inner world of imaginative speculation. Trying to answer them in the lives we lead could convert that inner world into a kingdom of principles. There we find ourselves in the presence of problems which touch our hearts on the occasions when we become our best selves. These are problems of right or wrong, of beauty or ugliness, of the existence or non-existence of God, of man's relation to Him and of His relation to man. They are infinitely complicated problems, and therefore they cannot be satisfactorily dealt with by the convenient rational mechanisms of the universities, by pure logical reasoning or by the distinctions that the higher learning has devised in dividing each problem into parts, and dealing with each part independently of the rest. It is possible, for example, in traditional political economy to solve, at least tentatively, what have been called specific problems of supply and demand by resorting to the abstraction which lifts the discussion out of the actual world, by assuming that "other things are equal." But in approaching the great issues that are decisive for an individual life—and societies are composed of individuals—other things are never equal. That is because happiness is whole. It depends upon appropriate harmonious relationships between all of a person's desires and hopes, together with the frustrations and the sadness which are inevitable parts of everyone's life. The theory of tangents and the calculus of probabilities helped Newton to set forth a single natural physical law pervading the universe; but mathematical concepts, no matter how refined, do not enable us to plot the curve of the deeper passions which govern human experience and determine what two persons shall be friends and what man and woman lovers.

The secrets of the heart concern us in the mysterious depths of our inner lives, especially when we are granted, as we so seldom are for valuable stretches of time, the absolute peace and quiet which all sensitive persons need for their growth. In so far as we are admitted, by our efforts and by grace, to a partial understanding of these secrets, we have a sense of participating in truth which transcends matter, space and time, in the search after which we are in some small degree the instruments of a higher purpose. If this inner life, by some mystery that science cannot fathom, transcends our bodily existence, if it links us to God, as the words of the Christian Gospel lead the believer to feel sure it does, then this inner life is our *lasting* possession. It is our true self. There it still is when the matter of which we are made disintegrates, because the truths, which through love and delight and virtue we share with God, are indestructible.

This inner life of the honest individual is also his most precious worldly possession; its radiation gives his bodily existence its joys and its sorrows, its sense of permanence. And if it be true, as the Christian faith suggests, that the course of our earthly sojourn determines our destiny, the decisions we make in the recesses of our inner lives have an apocalyptic significance that can raise all we think and do to a higher level of distinction. It is only in so far as our experiences and our conduct fortify this inner life, then, that we acquire the full sense of existing, of winning the victory over time, matter and space, and the evil inherent in all of them, which the dedicated person, so rare and so precious, feels bound to seek.

This need for the primacy of the spirit has been felt by many who are not Christian believers. The other day at a friend's apartment, I came on an old engraving of the chief of the revolutionary party at Lyons during the French Revolution, Joseph Chalier. He was a victim of the guillotine. In the inscription placed under his portrait, which apparently reproduces some of his words, this "martyr to liberty" recognizes the priority of the transcendental. "I bequeath my soul to Eternity," he says, "my heart to Patriots, and my body to brigands."

These words are too warlike, and, at least to my taste, too cynical about the body. With the hierarchy of values set forth in this inscription, the purpose of our worldly existence would be, it seems, to acquire valiant hearts and stout souls. But if violence is not tempered and controlled by compassion and charity, if courage is not guided by love, the soul is deprived of the elements that direct it towards eternity. Love alone can give life to beauty and to virtue, the love that consists in losing oneself in another, the love that is a gift of Christ. Samuel Johnson, who was mainly what would be called in our time a conservative and a nationalist, once spoke of patriotism as "the last refuge of a scoundrel." Therefore the heart is not properly the property of the patriots. It belongs to God, through the experiences of life that lead us to Him, because the attributes of the heart, at its best, are essential to enable the soul to join its Creator.

This book is called *A Search for Civilization.* Therefore I should make plain at the outset what meaning I attach to "civilization," and what relation a striving towards perfection by individuals, in their inner lives, has to the search. So far as students of history have been able to determine, the word "civilization" was introduced into language about the middle of the eighteenth century. It was apparently used first in French and very soon afterwards in English. It was invented to describe what was considered a new society in process of formation, a society believed by some of the most distinguished Europeans to be more enlightened and pacific than any of its predecessors.* It is in this sense, so different from the meaning widely given the word today, that it is used throughout this book.

If then "civilization" is, as it was to those who coined

* See below, p. 112.

8

the word, something in process of attainment, rather than something attained before and sometimes lost, the search we are conducting is for a better society than any known in history. The society we seek should serve the material needs of individuals, while raising them spiritually, by means of the love that is of God and which involves a giving of the self, to love their neighbors.

Can principles of universal validity be found, which men and women everywhere might come to accept as binding on themselves and on those who govern, principles which would help to keep hatred and jealousy within bounds? There is a profound sense in which such principles exist. They are stated in the words of Christ as these are recorded in the Gospel. Because of their divine origin and the infinite riches they contain, these words can often be interpreted only with difficulty, in relation to the specific cases with which men and women are confronted in their lives. In societies full of sin and corruption, their interpretation has been mainly confided to fallible, and sometimes sinful and corrupt persons, who have controlled the various churches founded, organized and administered in the name of Christ. Consequently the principles of the Gospel have not infrequently come to be identified, wrongly, with rigid rules and interpretations of rules, emanating at best only indirectly from God and at worst directly from self-interested men.

The fact that there are in the world today a number of competing religious institutions adds to the difficulties encountered by honest men who seek international understanding. The numerous divisions of the Christian faith, as well as the numerous other faiths, leave men without any shared foundation of commonly held ultimate beliefs, when such a foundation is an essential basis, not only for agreement, but for the constructive disagreement which can help provide the genuine unity of purpose indispensable to the coming of civilization.

In his recent essay on Goethe as a wise man, T. S. Eliot wrote: "Of revealed religions, and of philosophical systems, we must believe that one is right and the others wrong. But wisdom is . . . the same for all men everywhere." The difficulties of approaching persons who do not share one's religious beliefs in terms of these beliefs, are increased by the weaknesses of church government in the hands of mortal men, not a few of whom make the mistake, fatal to the search for wisdom, of thinking they have it in their keeping. That is why it is in terms of a search, based on the realization that the ultimate truths of the Gospel have always to be applied to particular changing conditions, that a Christian should strive to approach the overwhelmingly complex problems that confront the world today. Whatever their allegiance, the wisest sometimes find that a literal acceptance, as final arbiter in judgments of the mind, of all the rules of government established by the church to which they belong, involves them in commitments in the realm of ultimate belief that they are unable in their integrity to make. This is no less true for the judgments that originate in the imagination, that give intuitive insight into what is beautiful or ugly, good or bad, judgments that are needed to raise the rational process to a

10

higher, less inhuman plane than logical reasoning by itself, based as it is on positive knowledge, is capable of reaching. So it often comes about that even the tentative attainment of Christian ends depends not on a rigid adherence to rules and regulations of institutions, but on different interpretations from those usually given by uninspired officials. This is because the justice of God, unlike the justice of man, is never blind. It is always tempered by mercy and love. And the music of mercy and love is tolerance and patience.

The wisest men and women, therefore, fight shy of categorical assertions. They are instead, like Socrates, forever asking overwhelming questions, which provoke something approaching the right answers. As with Socrates, uncertainty rather than certainty is the symptom of their wisdom. Yet, in the critical moments of existence—as when the artist has to make his decisions, the lover to choose, the believer to face the consequences of his belief—they are more uncertain of their uncertainty than those who suppose they have found final answers are certain of their certainty. They recognize what it is they must do and what not do, and the chances are good that their decisions and their choices accord with the divine law, which is of God, and which the Gospel alone has expressed. Out of the works and the acts of dedicated, disinterested seekers after wisdom, rich materials might emerge fundamental for the growth of a world culture. In this way a search for wisdom by a few might help others to decide important issues that face them, in relation to the fresh problems and situations presented to us in these times of overwhelmingly rapid material changes. The great danger is that these changes will control men; the great need is for a search after wisdom to steer men through these changes. Such a search can contain an element of universality only when it is made by disinterested individuals.

In this sense wisdom may be spoken of as the major guide in the search for civilization, because it alone could enable men to find ultimate ends of life, which, without efforts to coerce, might inspire something approaching universal assent. Wisdom is not an alternative to faith, but a means of fortifying it. The words of Christ transmitted by the Gospel are divine law in its purest and final form. But it is only through wisdom in its application to concrete cases that the divine law can flourish in the temporal world and acquire the humanity and the universality that are its proper attributes.

During the War of 1939-45, the distinguished French man of letters, Georges Bernanos, spent a kind of exile in Brazil. He felt acutely the weaknesses of the Christian religion as practiced in his time, in the face of the totalitarianism which threatened, and in somewhat different forms still threatens, to debase men and women everywhere in an age when the supreme need is to elevate them as never before. In 1941, about a year after the German invasion of France, he wrote a moving letter to a French nun. Here are some essential passages:

"For many years now people have tried to fix the blame for the decadence of Christianity. They have failed because they looked in the wrong place; they looked outside Christianity, when those who are pri-

marily responsible are within. Mediocre Christians, mediocre priests are losing the world—smug Christians,
who are also, most often, sanctimonious property own-
ers. The Hitlerian power will founder like other dictator-
ships before it; and the world can repair everything material that has been lost. But only a miracle can save the
world's conscience. Two of the most illustrious Christian
societies of Europe—Italy and Spain—have already sur-
rendered to pagan realism spiritual values which were
not theirs to dispose of; they didn't own them; they are
the common property of mankind.

"Honor must be saved . . . honor must become Christian. The incredible divorce between heroism and honor
in the consciences of the youth, who are being misled
and made fanatical, must be prevented. Even if it possessed the richest churches, the most opulent clergy, and
the most immense privileges, a Christianity devoid of
honor would be nothing."*

Can the world's conscience be saved? Can honor,
which in earlier ages also has been often grievously
separated from the Founder, become Christian? Can
love, which is of God, replace force as the arbiter of
human destiny? Is such a miracle conceivable?

No one can answer. But many barriers that stand in
the way of civilization might be broken down if this were
recognized as *The Question,* to which all other questions
need to be referred. It is for individuals who recognize
the mission to which this question summons them, to

* I owe my knowledge of this letter to Jean and Corinne Désy.
Bernanos gave them a copy when Désy was Canadian ambassador to
Brazil.

try to answer in the work they do and the lives they lead. Individuals are capable of approaching closer than institutions to honor, love and charity. "Christ alone could say: I am the Truth," wrote Simone Weil. "No one else on earth has the right to say that, neither men nor collectivities, but institutions and other collectivities have even less right to say it than men. A man can sometimes attain such a degree of saintliness that Christ almost lives in him. But there is no such thing as a 'holy nation.'"°

That is why the greatest religious leaders, the greatest philosophers, the greatest artists—the greatest human beings wherever they appear—and they are not necessarily prominent, are always drinking at the fountain of wisdom. That fountain is accessible to everyone. It is denied only to those who exclude themselves. Without a recourse to it, honor, love and charity can hardly survive. With the help of wisdom they might increase and penetrate the fabric of industrialized life. Religion alone, as it exists today, cannot save these, the most precious of our possessions, which are God's gift to man. Nor can art, nor moral philosophy.

How then can wisdom penetrate those recognized realms of experience and help all three of them to interpenetrate for man's benefit, and through him for the benefit of civilization?

° Simone Weil, *L'enracinement,* Paris, 1949, p. 129.

CHAPTER II

Groups in its Service

IF "WISDOM is the same for all men everywhere," as Eliot suggests, it might provide cement capable of uniting races and nations in something approaching a universal community. The search for wisdom is not a profession like the work of the chemist, the banker or the engineer. It is not even a profession in the same sense as the work of the philosopher or the theologian, in spite of the comprehensive character of their subject matter compared with that of most other specialists. Has it then an object?

It certainly does not resemble the disciplines recognized and taught in schools and universities all over the world. Wisdom cannot be classified, filed or pinned "sprawling on a wall." It ceases when it becomes the monopoly of any man, or any group, or any special subject. The groups which might be formed to give it substance would lose it if they did anything to hoard it. Their service would depend on its cultivation and dissemination, and on their self-effacement. Often today, in the bedlam of excitement and hustle of economic endeavor, and also in the laboratories and cells where

15

university men set themselves off from life, even common sense seems to be nowhere. The mission of these groups would be to nourish the growth of common sense and humanity everywhere. For without them all is empty.

How can men spread them? Not mainly by rushing from place to place in rapid conveyances. For the members of such groups as we seek to create, the voyages had better arise out of the inner necessities of friendships. They should not be hurried and fleeting. "Don't dream of long journeys," wrote Saint Augustine, "go where you believe; it is not in navigating but in loving that one is drawn to Him who is everywhere." Such voyages have an important place in the itinerary of the rare statesman who has a heart and is seeking genuinely the peace of the world.

So wisdom (like charity according to the old saying) begins at home. It is inherent in the lives people lead with their families and in their callings, if those lives are good, those callings honorable and honest. Persons who seek to have it permeate their work and their life (and the prevalent notion that work and life are better kept in separate compartments seems to me false) can never make public appeals for virtue. They cannot formulate rules which others must follow. In every relationship of their lives they must avoid all smugness. Wisdom cannot be organized. If it is to lead towards universal principles, these can come only as a natural consequence of the search itself. Wisdom emerges only when it is a necessary part of the work a person does, when it springs for example out of what he writes, paints or composes, and out of what he says, especially under conditions of

agree with the leader seeking power, not under God, not for the sake of beauty and virtue, but solely for the sake of power. It is this misplaced allegiance to power, mingled with men's instinctive passion for violence, that has enabled communism to inspire a false heroism of the kind Bernanos, with the example of national socialism before him, described in his letter to the nun.

During the past hundred years there has been a recrudescence of the belief in force as the final arbiter of human destiny—a belief which some of the most influential of our eighteenth- and nineteenth-century ancestors thought might cease to predominate in international relations. This dependence on force has been strengthened by an unholy worship of the state as an end in itself, and by the rise of a cult of violence which makes force, for want of a nobler belief, appear peculiarly and unnaturally virtuous, as in the work of Georges Sorel. Communism, nazism and other forms of totalitarianism have fed on these sources. In the case of communism, the *mistique* of violence has been combined with what appears to the naive to be a more exalted concept. The absolute form of government is made an expression of mass will; the mass will (by force of numbers) is represented as superior in the human benefit it makes possible to the individual will, no matter how wise and loving the individual may be. In this way communism is represented as the best means of making the poor and the miserable happy. It is out of these ingredients, at the service of the egotism of ambitious individuals, that totalitarianism in general and communism in particular have gained so many adherents in the twentieth century.

18

Materialism, in its various forms, originated to a considerable extent out of a desire to provide the human being with a new dignity, by no means narrowly economic in character. The idea was that material improvement would improve people in every way, help them to be more virtuous, to create beauty, even to serve and to love their fellows better. This idea contains a measure of truth.* Without the hope and confidence that it bred in some of the best and most influential Europeans and Americans during the seventeenth and eighteenth centuries, industrialism could hardly have triumphed so rapidly in Europe and North America. In so far as this idea is at the root of the satisfaction derived from mounting figures of production and of income, that satisfaction is morally much more elevated than the satisfaction derived from the worship of mass rule. But the idea has never had a very solid basis in experience. Unmitigated materialism, which is no monopoly of the communists, debases the human being. It tends to make him worse than he naturally is, in an epoch when, as never before, there is a supreme need for him to be better. For only if he is better, much better, which means also self-effacing, can individualism lead effectively to higher goals than communism.

The connection which originally existed between better human beings and human beings who are better off, has been weakened in recent times in the West itself. Vulgarity, bad taste and cheapness have acquired a respectability that they lacked in the lives of those few who were well off one and two centuries ago. So the prevalent materialistic conception of the purpose of life

* See below, chap. 8.

among the Western peoples does not provide an adequate answer to totalitarianism. Moreover the avowed purposes of the two forms of materialism—the communistic and the democratic—seem to be growing more and more alike, especially now that Russia and China put forward claims to world supremacy on the basis of the same kinds of impressive statistics of production and income, the same kinds of technical mastery and specialized knowledge, which the Western peoples once alone possessed.

The making of better human beings is a personal not a mass matter; it is a matter of excellence not of uniformity; it grows out of individual responsibility and effort, not out of techniques of mass education and mechanized social improvement. The present weakness of materialism is explained by the fact that it fails to nourish excellence in the human being beyond his special field of endeavor, and the fragmentation of fields of endeavor into ever more numerous specialties has been by no means generally accompanied by greater scope in each for the human capacity of dedicated and creative workmanship. The ideals of individual achievement and disinterested independence, associated to a considerable extent with materialism from the seventeenth to the nineteenth century, have been increasingly submerged in egotism.

There is nothing new, of course, in the desire of individuals to serve themselves rather than their neighbors. Miserliness of every kind was a grievous fault of many of our Christian ancestors, and there is some evidence, in the willingness of the rich to give, that the love of money for its own sake is now less prevalent in the United States than it was both in Europe and America in the earlier phases of industrialism, and all over the world before its rise. But ample giving is usually organized. It is done through agents, through foundations. Men are paid to extract and to give other people's money. Thus the gifts lose personal meaning.

The need for charity in the deeper sense, which money or material goods by themselves are powerless to supply, the need for outgoingness, for giving one's self, is now greater than it ever was, as a result of the increasingly impersonal nature of human relations. There is only one way to overcome egotism and that is by unselfish love, and the opportunities for loving do not seem to have kept pace at all with the rapid increase in production and in speed of movement and communication.

Egotism is more insidious than ever. It is easier for any naive person, with good will, to deny its existence because it is now more difficult than it used to be to distinguish from altruism. During the early twentieth century, with the spread of psychiatry and psychoanalysis, the practice of analyzing people's motives acquired an allegedly scientific validity which it had lacked before; meanwhile the prestige of science has grown. At the same time there has been a weakening in the belief in firm moral values.

These developments have given steam to the spread of the cynical notion that a man is incapable of acting altruistically, that even when he appears to be doing so he is indulging in some form of self-expression or self-love, that the motives of good and evil are so mixed up

21

in most actions that it becomes futile to consider any action in moral terms. At the same time Marxianism and Freudianism have been widely interpreted as indicating that individual actions are determined mainly by forces over which a person has no control. Both developments have made it more difficult to hold individuals responsible for their acts.

Of course all men fall short of perfection in their attempts to serve the beautiful, the good, the enduring. It is also true that the efforts men make, in striving to do their work well, lead many to become pretentious and prideful. Perfectionism, trying to achieve the impossible, is always a danger. But the greater danger now is the failure to distinguish it from an honest striving to do one's best in one's relations with one's fellows. The shortcomings and the weaknesses of those who seek perfection in their inner lives ought not to discredit the search. The search cannot be delegated to others. No one but the self can make decisions that concern the soul.

In the United States nothing perhaps has made individual efforts to serve the good appear so useless as the widespread impression, to which I have just alluded, that the quest for inner perfection is nothing but a form of egotism. It has become increasingly common, as instruction of the young has grown more and more practical, to confuse the deeper values with mere activity, to confuse the good with a dehumanized synthetic altruism, to forget that the cultivation of the quiet family virtues, the virtues of housekeeping, provides a solid basis for any effective activities helpful to others. I remember a high school teacher who followed some advanced courses at the University of Chicago concerned with philosophical ideas. She was patient for a time, but finally became exasperated and declared that we would all do better to get out and deliver milk in the poorer quarters of Chicago than to waste our time in futile speculation concerning the good, the true and the beautiful.

Certainly direct economic help to the needy is exacting and meritorious; but its merits are of a different order from the more private effort to arouse in students a love of lasting values, to create a work of art, or to make one's relations with one's wife or husband into something approaching a work of living art. Furthermore, the coming of an economy of abundance in the United States, combined with "organized charity" plus social security, has rendered the beneficent activities which this high school teacher invoked less necessary than they were in the nineteenth century.

It is easy to dismiss this high school teacher's remark as misguided. Yet I have the impression that it partially reflects, in a naive form, a concern over the disappearance of personal warmth in human relations. This concern has a real foundation. With the uniform treatment of the sick and needy and the encroachment of public on private life which have accompanied the rapid material growth of recent decades, much of the compassion and consolation that was possible a generation or two ago has been squeezed out of human relations. Technological progress and the increasing scale of enterprise not only make it possible to do away with thousands of persons in concentration camps in an impersonal way,

23

but now to slaughter millions by missiles set in motion by persons who do not see the victims. The collectivities—both private and public—which have taken over the distribution of funds for education and for relieving material want, facilitate a dehumanized egotism. There is something almost equally inhuman in feeding *en masse*, in raising wages *en masse*, in subsidizing and reforming education *en masse* and in killing *en masse*. These insidious consequences that have come with rapid economic growth have been accompanied by a tendency to make the interest of the group or the enterprise or the agency to which one belongs, the ultimate objective of those who direct groups, enterprises and agencies. Thus a labor union leader claims that his success in defeating management in the industry is of general benefit to the nation. Thus a president of a huge corporation confuses the success of his enterprise with the general welfare of his country, or even of the world. Up to a point the competition reflected by this kind of confusion is inevitable. It is even desirable in so far as it stimulates production in the industrialized world of our times. But the destruction of personal relationships based on integrity, the absence of values transcending organized collectivities, shrivel up the very qualities that made possible the coming of these huge enterprises and the accompanying material successes of the past hundred and fifty years.

A consequence has been to make all improvement in the character of individuals seem useless. This result is certainly not Christian in origin, but it has become more and more widespread among the peoples of Christian origin, whose best men and women once set an example. It has been accompanied by organized movements for moral rearmament, which are in the main dismaying. Organized virtue, like organized wisdom, is a contradiction in terms. It can become a means of destroying the real virtue for which men and women everywhere are starved, and which can only be personal, which does not come from a sense of guilt but from a love of giving. What is needed is the quiet inconspicuous practice of decency in all the public and private domains of life, so that it comes to be a habit, not to be talked or sermonized about, but lived.

What have been the results of the abdication of personal responsibility for ultimate values? Political and artistic, even religious and moral issues (when they arise) have been pushed aside for the practical success of some special interest. A man is seldom inspired to direct his activities towards truth, beauty or justice, which he can do only by subordinating himself and his interests to a higher, nobler purpose. He considers instead only the degree of utility he finds in making a choice on behalf of "my" business, "my" labor union, "my" university, "my" special field, "my" church, and me. Collective selfishness has replaced individual selfishness as a force in societies. Collective selfishness is less personal, but it is difficult to discover that it inflicts less spiritual suffering or that disinterestedness has gained from the change. Nor, it would seem, have graciousness and charm. With the decline in the sense of individual responsibility, and the abandonment of the older cultural values of good taste and workmanship, vulgarity,

25

ordinariness have become primary factors in history to a degree that was hardly true among the Western peoples in the immediate past.

The spread of comforts and physical facilities have not fully offset the forces making for vulgarity. The facilities for cleanliness offer fresh possibilities for the development of taste but, in the main, they have not been happily exploited because of what appears to be a decline in taste itself. The strength of what I have called the materialistic conception of the purpose of civilization, as it evolved in Europe in the seventeenth and eighteenth centuries, rested to no small extent on the quality, the beauty of the commodities produced. The fashioning of such commodities required a high order of skill and art. In this way it provided the fulfillment which only difficult, varied and sustained labor can bring. Today workmen, in most callings, expect to receive a larger remuneration for very much less effort, and for effort that requires less fortitude—less spiritual, moral and aesthetic strength—than did much of the work performed during the seventeenth, eighteenth and nineteenth centuries. That work was mostly honest and pure, whatever the moral shortcomings of those who did it. There is less in today's work—save in that done by persons who stand aside from the regular channels of employment and housekeeping, and even the regular channels of leadership—that inspires the imagination and elicits the creative energy of man.

To meet the menace of totalitarianism and the barbarism that have invaded even Western countries in the twentieth century, human nature needs affirmations based on deep knowledge, thought and belief, and sustained by enthusiastic and firmly directed action. What most men have been offered instead is negations or superficial appeals wrapped mostly in worn-out slogans. Words have been misspoken until they have often lost the meanings they once possessed, and with those, all meaning of value. Inspiring words such as liberty and equality and civilization have been frequently turned inside out. In the midst of the noise which is now pumped into public gathering places, homes, automobiles, parks and once quiet hillsides, it is little wonder that more sublime words, such as charity, compassion and love, are rarely recognized for the possibilities they contain.

With such conditions as prevail, the suggestion that men should seek a common understanding of the purposes of existence seems to most of them unintelligible. With the divisions and subdivisions of work and interest that predominate, universal purpose is the last thing that men and women have in their minds. Absence of ultimate purpose has tended during the past half century to be confused, in the United States at any rate, with a false notion of freedom, for example in the education of the young. It is still common, though less so than between the two World Wars, to suppose that a democratic education consists in leaving all children free to do what they please, without realizing that the supreme joy of knowing what to do for the spiritual fulfillment that benefits our race comes only under exceptionally fortunate circumstances to a few persons later in their lives. Actually no one of us can be free to do what he pleases.

27

The freedom of the individual is restricted in every moment of his life, at least by his physical and psychical constitution, by the size of his income, and even by his freedom, if freedom is offered him without his knowing what to do with it. As an ultimate aim the emancipation of the individual isn't even a happy dream. It can condemn him to one of the worst forms of slavery, slavery to himself. When a man is left to choose, without an ideal beyond himself to inspire his choice, all the values that he needs to strengthen himself are likely to drown in the multiplicity of choices existent in the complicated hurried world promoted by industrialism. If he lacks a hierarchy of values, such a man is incapable of making a choice that will satisfy even him. "Must I do what I want to?" a young child, her eyes full of tears, asked one of her teachers, after having spent some months in a school where the children were urged to follow their own inclinations and so to educate themselves.

Freedom consists in choosing the right slavery. The true road to freedom is the road of love, and, as we have just said, the only means of loving is to forget oneself. Love is the highest form of slavery.

The false conception that freedom consists in leaving a child, or in leaving oneself, free to do anything one likes (whatever pleases one's ego, whatever is to one's material advantage) has been accompanied by another false conception which might seem to the unwary a strong counterweight to the first. It is the assumption that a man's life is at the mercy of material circumstances. When his conduct is determined on the basis of that assumption, he is relieved of effort in ways that tend

28

to make his existence both insidious and perfidious. He mistakes the freedom that he finds in submitting to what he thinks is inevitable, for the true freedom that can come only into the dedicated life of a person who has found the grace of loving something nobler and greater than himself. In the latter case the inevitability of the choices he makes comes from rising out of his ego; in the former from sinking farther into it. Like the notion that freedom is furthered by doing whatever one pleases, the notion that one's life is determined by material circumstances relieves a man of responsibility for serving ends that are beyond himself. In serving his own ends in this narrow way he becomes profoundly unhappy.

Under the joint influence of these two conceptions, which complement and promote at the same time that they contradict and offset one another, the schoolteachers, who share in bringing up the young, and the scholars, who provide the new knowledge that is sought in the hope that it will correct and amplify the subject matter upon which the teachers draw, have helped to establish a new view of the possible ways in which the human being can fill his life as an individual. This view is prevalent among the educationists and the scholars, and those who go in for what is called the "intellectual life" as a side line; in short the very persons who in the modern world are supposed to have culture in their keeping. It consists in believing that men and women can fulfill themselves, exercise their freedom, in two possible ways.

The first is to affirm the Self. A person can do this in

a variety of roles as a consumer. For example a man or woman is free to exercise his powers in choosing between various standardized breakfast foods, washing machines, ready-made dresses, electric refrigerators, cigarettes or automobiles, radio and television programs. These choices are sometimes not without value, but the possibilities of choice are limited, and mostly mechanical. They are not of the kind that require for full satisfaction any very active participation, save in the case of the automobile, and here the amount is continually reduced by the facilities that service stations provide and by the automatic driving devices that the motor companies install. The liberty of action in such affirmations of the Self provides small scope for creative imagination, or even for personal delight.

Another widely accepted way to affirm the Self consists in the right of the student or scholar or college graduate to choose his vocation or, if he goes into university education, his subject of research. Such freedom might have much value for the formation of a rich personality if it were conceived in a different way. But in the present epoch, with the emphasis that is laid on specialization and material success, a person soon finds himself in a groove. There he has, or at least thinks he has, opportunities for work only within areas where his choices have less and less to do with the deeply human problems which alone can nourish a rich inner life. There is little or nothing to stimulate those rare sensitive persons, who are disinterested and potentially inventive, seriously to apply themselves to the issues of life as a whole. So their imaginative faculties dry up. At the very time when a man achieves a professional success, he becomes prematurely old.

My historical inquiries have convinced me that it is individuals, with their decisions and their personal engagements as men and women, far more than mass movements, that determine history. As Simone Weil expresses it: "Personal sentiments play a rôle in human events that is never fully apparent. The fact that there is, or is not, a friendship between two men, or between two groups, can under certain circumstances prove decisive for human destiny." But the false conceptions of freedom that have taken possession of men and women in what is often called the free world stand in the way of making wisdom a greater force in the search for civilization.

The values which laid the cultural foundations for industrial civilization have lost their strength during the past hundred years.* Everyone is so busy doing his special work and receiving his synthetic amusement, that there is virtually no encouragement for the creative thoughts and actions that are so needed. The discoveries of the rare searcher after wisdom have been replaced by the makers of slogans, based on superficial knowledge and superficial experience. Billy Sunday, Aimee Semple McPherson and Billy Graham succeed one another in their exhortations to large crowds. They are soon forgotten. They are possibly devoid of bad intentions, but their cries are devoid of deep understanding, of all that is authentic and lasting in the heart. By assembling large

* Compare my *War and Human Progress,* Cambridge (Mass.), 1950, part iii.

audiences they color and affect the lives of very many. These people are led consequently to suppose that the only gifts capable of providing spiritual sustenance, in realms of universal significance, are charged with violent emotion, are separated from reason and from genuine imaginative insight, and from the deeper love which is far removed from passing fancy and which unlike simulated love cannot be accompanied by hatred. Insight and reason, at their best, have to be personal and intimate. Those qualities which human beings now so greatly need, both for their individual salvation and for the collective salvation of the race, cannot be distributed in labeled packages like soap, cigarettes or tickets of admission to baseball games and prize fights.

Is there any way out of the blind alley produced by mechanization and automation and the education which concerns itself mainly with man in the mass, with the uniformities which diminish the possibilities for excellence? In many persons who are young in spirit, and often also in years, there is a deep hunger for a fresh start. And with the powers of production which science and technology have released, our epoch might offer unprecedented possibilities for creative minds and dedicated hearts concerned with the part they can have in guiding human destiny. If such individuals can find others of their kind, great opportunities are open to them. Hope seems to lie in the formation of small independent groups of persons of good will, of established position, distinguished and disinterested and concerned, out of the depths of wide knowledge and firsthand experience, with the values that are of critical importance if societies are to live together more peacefully than in the past. These groups should draw into them as associates, by the hope and the enthusiasm they are able to generate, younger men and women of exceptional promise and exceptional independence, who have not been made to conform by specialization or the pursuit of their advantage, and who feel the need for firm values. Such groups can only accomplish their aims if they are formed spontaneously by a few individuals who have confidence in the integrity of the others. They would be groups of friends, who believe that their work and that of their fellow members will be strengthened by the opportunities afforded for a closer and more intimate community of experience and thought than is possible without such a marriage of common shared purposes. Organized publicity would be likely to jeopardize the purity of their influence. It needs to be achieved through their publications and by the direct relations they have, both as individuals and as members of their group, with men of action, with the leaders in diplomacy, politics, business and art, who are their friends and who seek their counsel.

They would not divorce themselves from the world, but would strive to bring the higher standards of thought and conduct that they share to bear concretely on its practical problems. For instance they would hold colloquies, lasting a week or so, on such subjects as these: The ways to diminish the possibilities of war with nuclear weapons. The future of education and of the higher learning as a basis for the improvement of the individual and for more enlightened and compassionate leadership. The reform of international relationships and associates of these groups, could help raise firm barriers against dictatorship, merciless violence and total war, by the emphasis laid on the purposes of civilized life and by the creation of ideals of grandeur based on love and compassion rather than on power. Channels could be opened to a wide public by enlightened publishers of newspapers and popular magazines and by enlightened directors of radio and television programs. In this way such groups could provide courts of appeal— means throughout the world of fortifying individuals who are hungry for the honest and the authentic.

Love of the neighbor, love even of one's enemies, the love that is given its deepest meaning by Our Lord, has become a necessity for the survival of the civilization our ancestors managed to establish. If the search for wisdom can give a sense of concrete reality to the highest ends of civilized life, in connection with the specific problems with which societies and organizations, as well as individuals, are concerned, if it can relate all current issues to ultimate principles, this search might transform the ways of life and the spirit of educational, political and religious institutions. Thus wisdom offers hope for a better, more decent society than has ever existed, at the time when such a society, to be decent, has to be universal.

The saving of civilization is bound to be full of difficulties that seem insuperable. Efforts to bring wisdom to count more than it ever has before in the great decisions which determine events, are bound to be misunderstood. They are utopian. When a person sets foot on this road, he is likely to be overwhelmed with a consciousness of his unworthiness for the task, especially since it involves him in offering, by implication, advice, as well as example, to others. If this does not make him feel humble, he has no place on the road. But, if it does, he has the duty to persist because the road that wisdom indicates is the road of hope. Utopia has become, to a degree that was never before true, the only practical guide for the plight in which suffering human beings everywhere find themselves.

In what directions should we look, then, in seeking the routes to Utopia? To what realms of human experience is wisdom applicable? Where shall we find the principles capable of drawing human beings of all nations and creeds, of all races and conditions, to recognize common purposes higher than themselves?

mainly with the history or the methods of philosophers and theologians, but of those who are actually striving to deal as individuals with the cosmic and often agonizing issues which confront them today. If such persons occupy positions of authority, or if they are in a position to move others who do, they have a chance to influence the great decisions for the good of man. So, for better or for worse, they help to prepare man's future.

That is why anyone concerned with fundamental philosophical or theological issues ought to address himself to the imagination, the sensibility and the conscience of his hearers and his readers. If he is to do so effectively, he ought to speak and write in a language which is at the same time elevated and intelligible. He should aim to reach tentative conclusions that touch the depths of any sensitive person's inner being, and present them in such a way that any sensitive person who is willing to make an effort can understand and be moved by them.

How few are the philosophers who have spoken in that way! What has helped the works of Plato and Epictetus, and even Aristotle, to endure is their style, the simplicity their authors managed to achieve in treating the greatest and most general issues of experience. Pascal recognized that a truth badly expressed has little chance of survival. No doubt the best-known modern philosophers discuss momentous matters of personal life, but their formulas are so austere, their ideas are phrased in such forbidding, such abstract, language, that they often mystify and disconcert more than they enlighten and please. They seldom make a gift of the truths they believe they have fathomed, in a spirit that is sufficiently intimate to touch the heart. Modern philosophers and their students seem to belong, more than the great classical philosophers, to a sort of esoteric club which exhibits Greek letters rather than the clarity that was Greek.

During recent years, with successive industrial revolutions and the triumph of industrialism, the breach between the accredited philosophical treatises and the sensibility of the reasonable, decent person seems to have widened. I have been asking myself why. Recently an explanation came to me while reading some lectures which Sir Eric Ashby published in 1958 called *Technology and the Academics*. He explains that teachers of philosophy in the universities demonstrate, what is to him perhaps their greatest merit, a no less rigorous objectivity and detachment in handling evidence than most natural scientists.

There is no disputing that objectivity is indispensable in philosophical speculations, but is the objectivity that is needed of the same kind which is required in the natural sciences? Is not the disinterestedness appropriate to philosophy more akin to that demonstrated by the artist, which I attempt to describe in a later chapter?* The personality and the inner life of the individual have never been made effectively part of the subject matter studied in the natural sciences or in mathematics. But the personality and inner life of the individual are an essential part of the philosopher's subject matter. Consequently indifference concerning the religious, aesthetic or moral significance of the results obtained, which is in-

* See below, pp. 174 ff.

39

evitable in dealing with the subjects of natural science, is misplaced in philosophy. It is not enough for the philosopher to think straight. He must talk straight and write straight, as Aristotle tried to do, in behalf of what is good for man, and through the individual man for mankind.

The proper subject of philosophical inquiry is human beings, not simply as bodies but as souls. Men and women are almost infinitely more complicated and richer in humanity than the objects of scientific inquiry, even when the scientist is a philosophically-inclined biologist (like Julian Huxley or C. H. Waddington) dealing with bodily life and its meaning for societies. It is therefore of mighty import for the student of philosophy on which side truth is found. If the philosophical inquirer is indifferent about the capacity of the individual to serve the true, the beautiful and the good, he is either evil or inhuman. That is why the philosopher, to be equal to his calling, has to maintain his detachment in the presence of a preference for those potentialities which elevate rather than debase human nature. His is properly an enlisted objectivity, because he is dealing with human attributes over which an individual can have some control, such as he can hardly have at all, or can have only with great difficulty, over natural processes like changes in the weather or the onset of disease. The more complete detachment which is possible for the scientist is a luxury the philosopher ought not to permit himself.

There is a further difference between the approaches to truth made by the natural scientist and by the philosopher or the theologian. A distinguished scientist, who is a recognized master in metallurgy both from the historical and the theoretical point of view, recently discussed with me the evolution of science since the sixteenth century. He suggested that the dazzling success which modern scientists have achieved has been possible because the problems they have set themselves to solve have been increasingly simple. He went on to point out that the problems which now cry for solution are problems of immense and growing complexity. Indeed the solutions of scientific problems, because of the complications that they have brought into human relations, have in some ways made it increasingly difficult to deal with personal problems. The rational processes now accepted as valid scientifically, which began to be applied between about 1570 and 1650, and whose adoption constituted what is now frequently called "the scientific revolution," can perhaps give us, as they have been and continue to be exploited, all the positively verifiable truths that man can ever need concerning the physical and biological universe. But the fullest knowledge in those domains is incomplete knowledge. Modern scientific methods—the positive test by experimental evidence, the increasingly accurate measurement of tangible phenomena, the almost incredible refinements of mathematics—are always inadequate to the treatment of great philosophical and theological issues.

During the past thirty years or so some of the most eminent scientists have recognized the limitations of modern scientific methods, as well as of modern scientific results. I have in mind men such as Schrödinger, Whitehead, Sherrington, Whittaker, Hubble. I think all

41

of them would find themselves in agreement with what Schrödinger wrote on this subject in his recent book, *Nature and the Greeks.*

"Science," he said, "represents the level best we have been able to ascertain in the way of safe and incontrovertible knowledge. . . . [Yet] I am . . . astonished that the scientific picture of the real world around me is very deficient. . . . It is ghastly silent about all and sundry that is really near to our heart, that really matters to us. . . . It knows nothing of God and Eternity, good or bad, beautiful and ugly. Science sometimes pretends to answer questions in these domains, but the answers are very often so silly that we are not inclined to take them seriously.

"So, in brief, we do not belong to this material world that science constructs for us. We are not in it. . . . We believe that we are in it [because] . . . our bodies belong to [it]. . . ."°

If the life of the body appears to so many men today to exhaust the real world, this is partly because their inner lives are barren. The world they move in *is* an unreal world in so far as the deeper experiences are concerned. How then can we learn more about the other world which, as Schrödinger's words suggest, means so much to all of us?

On the eve of the Second World War the great astronomer, Edwin Hubble, distinguished in lectures he gave at the University of California between what can be known scientifically and what cannot. Science, he wrote,

° Edwin Schrödinger, *Nature and the Greeks,* Cambridge, 1954, pp. 93-96.

explores "the public domain of positive knowledge." There remains, he said, "the private domain of personal judgments." Hubble adds that in this domain, which Schrödinger considers the real world, "each man acquires his own wisdom from his own experience."

What are personal judgments? What is a man's "own wisdom"? Does it differ from wisdom? Whence has come the widely held opinion, which Hubble's words express, that "wisdom" is devoid of universality, when the position in the Middle Ages of Christian philosophers, many of whom admired and utilized the works of the most famous Greeks, was that in the domain where personal judgments alone are applicable, universal and immutable truths can be discovered? And also that any sensible man, whatever his training and vocation, can verify these truths; that a law of reason, as Richard Hooker wrote in the late sixteenth century, "is not agreed upon by one, or two, or few, but by all."*

The change in the idea of the nature of truth, that accompanied and followed "the scientific revolution," seems to come from a philosophical tendency which can be traced back at least as far as Thomas Hobbes, who was born in 1588—the year of the Armada—about the time Hooker was writing the *Laws of Ecclesiastical Polity*. Hobbes and many other modern philosophers have supposed, without *scientific* proof, that different men's inner experiences, some of which provide the stuff of wisdom, have no common source, that man's relation to God, if he has one, does not enable him to participate

* Richard Hooker, *Of the Laws of Ecclesiastical Polity* (1592-94) Book I, chap. viii, sec. 9.

in any form of being which is independent of matter, space and time. The holders of this view are left without faith in the possibility of communicating fully the essentials of their inner experiences or of believing that there can be anything immutable about the truths men are capable of comprehending. With the extension of this philosophical outlook in modern times, learned men have come more and more to believe, as Hubble did, that no "personal judgment" can have an objective value comparable to an established scientific proposition, that it cannot belong in "the public domain of positive knowledge" no matter how deep and serious is the experience on which it is based, or how honest and discerning its author may be in reaching it.

Such an outlook concerning the nature of truth leaves all discoveries, which are not verifiable by scientific methods, projections of the self. Truth has thereby been harnessed to those natural processes which a man can observe, explain and utilize for practical purposes, but over which he has, as a scientist, little or no aesthetic or moral control. This leads to a denial that any statement concerning what Schrödinger calls the "real world" can be disinterested. Such a denial makes it difficult for two human beings to understand each other and interferes with the achievement of anything approaching spiritual union. The individual is alone. He is left without common roots in eternity at the very time when the triumph of industrialism, by sweeping him away from the soil, has deprived him of such bodily roots as his ancestors had in the temporal world. It is no wonder that on a planet where science and technology have brought al-

44

most all human beings into interdependence, where most people see in a day many more people than a medieval peasant saw in a year, the individual is generally more lonely than his ancestors.

> Many of one mouth, of one breath,
> Dressed as one,—and none brothers among them.*

To the extent it is denied that the deepest personal experiences of one person can correspond fully, in their differences as well as in their resemblances, to those of another, the possibility is diminished for the most moving of all exchanges, the merging of two lives. The possibilities for constructive friendship are lessened. Marriage can never be complete. This has deep consequences for faith. If the search for wisdom is nothing more than a private experience, if the verification of judgments can never be essentially the same for two persons, no place is left for wisdom as a means of striving towards objective truth. Wisdom is relegated to the domain of solitary opinion. That is what the distinguished Spanish philosopher Unamuno seems to have had in mind when he wrote, early in the twentieth century, that "science is the enemy of wisdom."

But application of wisdom to questions of belief and of devotion seems necessary for the establishment of civilization on firm philosophical foundations. If the universal validity of wisdom is denied, faith is left blind, without possible rational justification. So is love.

___

* Archibald MacLeish, "American Letter," in *New Found Land*, Paris, 1930.

Schrödinger's statement suggests that the real world, which the natural sciences are incapable of revealing and helping us to understand, comprises the realms of God and eternity, beautiful and ugly, good and bad. It comprises, therefore, the realms of love and hatred, concerning which the natural sciences are equally silent. These are all domains into which the search for wisdom must penetrate. Unless that search is recognized as the same for all men everywhere, which Eliot's words proclaim it to be, the chance for a deep community of belief among the peoples of the world is denied. Unless the possibility exists, through wisdom, of discovering common good in faith, in beauty and in virtue, there can hardly be a genuine entente among the members of our race. It is in their inner lives that human beings seek for the permanent. The vital matter is that their inner experiences should be the source not of loneliness but of communion, not of hatred but of love.

The imagination and the heart, like the mind, have powers of transcendence which the body lacks. They do not alter in the same ways or to the same extent as does the body. A rich inner life need not diminish with age. It can gain in resourcefulness. This we see in those rare older people who are the salt of the earth. They are younger in their minds, and especially in their hearts and imaginations, than they were before. Madame de Sévigné's relative was thinking of this when, late in her life, he told her that men and women divide in two categories: those who ought never to have been born and those who ought never to die.

This is a spiritual distinction, meaningless unless man has a personal relationship to God. The great Greeks of

46

antiquity already sensed its truth when they invented the saying, "Whom the gods love die young." By those words they seem to have meant that those old who ought never to die, are younger and freer in spirit than ever before. It is the power of rising out of oneself, of giving for love of another, of accepting even solitude because when one is solitary one is not alone, that has created the greatest artists, the wisest men, the most saintly characters and the most perfect lovers.

Few manage to forget themselves; they are the happy few. They possess something that all men and women wish for, however much they conceal their desires from themselves. Their discoveries in living have a permanent reality, like the greatest art, because both are related to God Himself, towards Whom the human being is haltingly but honestly drawn, and because they are presented in forms which, unlike the discoveries of the natural scientist, are partly independent of the material world that will pass away. Saint Augustine wrote that God made time, and is therefore beyond it. Our relationship to God makes it possible for us too, in our work and our love, to become partly independent of time.

What kind of world is it that science reveals, the world of which only our bodies are part? Does it reveal even the whole of that world? The new knowledge concerning nature and the body is very great indeed and is continually increasing. It teaches us much about the ways to take care of ourselves and others. But it is knowledge of special kinds which have limitations of their own so far as the ways we understand ourselves are concerned. Almost everything that we experience directly with our senses has been pillaged by the new natural

47

sciences since the times of Galileo (1564-1642). I say pillaged because these tangible materials of substances, of space, of time have been examined in special ways, in terms of abstractions which scientists have discovered in their amazingly successful efforts to explain the behavior of natural phenomena of every sort, prominent among them the behavior of the body in health and in disease. Those abstractions have realities of their own but these realities do not kindle insight concerning other realities which need to be explored if human beings are to understand one another.

The kinds of rigorous inquiry which have enabled men and women to prolong their lives so astonishingly, have been accomplished by a focusing of attention on certain attributes of matter, space and time. As Eddington pointed out years ago, the scientist considers objects in ways that differ from their appearance. These are partial attributes. They do not correspond to the sense impressions of daily life. What is real for him in his role of scientist is *unreal* or irrevelant to him in his role of man. "One had to be Newton," wrote Paul Valéry, "to observe the moon is falling when anyone can see for himself it isn't falling."* This difference between what the individual searches for as a scientist (often now as the member of a team), and what he discovers as a man, helps to explain why there is hardly a modern description of the behavior of a person in disease which will strike the responsive reader as so living as that of Hippocrates, the great Greek doctor who dwelt and practiced

* Cited by Louis de Broglie, *Savants et découvertes*, Paris, 1951, p. 34.

twenty-five hundred years ago. Hippocrates looked on the body from the point of view of an artist rather than of a scientist, and the artist at his best reveals what we recognize when we see it, and preserves this for all to recognize.

The change in outlook which was brought about by modern science and which pervades the contemporary world came decisively with William Harvey (1578-1657). It has many consequences for medicine and surgery. One is the habit of considering as of public interest, not concrete individual cases but general averages of life expectancy or of the incidence of particular diseases. Today the scientific doctor, for instance a great obstetrician like the late I. B. Rubin, analyzes sickness in his published works in terms of the average morbidity. He classifies cases where Hippocrates or Phidias dealt with particular persons. It is the *category*, not the individual, that is treated as scientifically interesting and important.

In employing his senses in the often exciting and successful search after novel scientific results, a scholar therefore misses certain most important values as they arise out of the same concrete objects and bodies that provide the artist with his materials. The scientist does not, in his role as scholar, experience the magic and wonder of a sunset, of fresh fallen snow whitening the dark branches of trees. Least of all does he value in his role as scientist the supreme magic and wonder of a beautiful woman. No doubt atoms have their beauties, but he is a perverse man who would want to make love to them.

The outlook of the modern natural scientist, in concentrating on such tangible aspects of human beings as the physiological and atomical composition of their bodies, has influenced us to experience and to consider tangible experiences in terms of these abstractions. Of itself, therefore, scientific progress does little to direct men and women towards moral and spiritual judgments, or to guide them towards beauty and virtue, or towards love. It is beyond the range of the natural sciences to penetrate the realm of our most profound hopes.

Universities and institutes of research today possess much prestige, because there is a disposition, more perhaps in the Anglo-Saxon than in the Latin countries, to presume that men with doctor's degrees and academic posts have the monopoly of knowledge. We are told that ninety per cent of all the great men who have ever lived are alive today, but few even of the best informed persons know why they are great, and none know even the names of all of them. The prestige attached to what are called "the intellectuals," therefore, is largely abstract, arising as it does among the public from the growing size and number of the universities, and the extension of instruction to practical subjects.* It is based less than in the Latin countries on a respect for the professor's calling as such.

What then is the nature of the knowledge derived from the higher learning? No one perhaps has described it better than the late A. N. Whitehead. Celebrated mathematician that he was, he wrote out of wide and

---

* I have discussed this subject in a paper, "Is the Intellectual Life an End in Itself?" published in the January 1962 number of *The Review of Politics.*

prolonged experience as a professor in Great Britain and the United States.

"The seventeenth century," Whitehead says, ". . . produced a scheme of scientific thought framed by mathematicians, for the use of mathematicians. The chief characteristic of the mathematical mind is its capacity for dealing with abstractions; and for eliciting from them clear-cut demonstrative trains of reasoning, entirely satisfactory so long as it is those abstractions which you want to think about." This world of scientific abstractions makes even nature "a dull affair," he says, "soundless, senseless, colourless; merely the hurrying of material, endlessly, meaninglessly." "Every university in the world," he adds, "organizes itself in accordance with . . . the characteristic scientific philosophy which closed the seventeenth century. . . . No alternative system of organizing the pursuit of scientific truth has been suggested. It is not only reigning, but it is without a rival. And yet—it is quite unbelievable."*

The learned scholars, who move about in this world of scientific abstractions, have usurped for their "unbelievable" results what Whitehead calls a "misplaced concreteness." They have often mistaken their abstractions for realities. It follows that the kinds of truths which have come to be regarded as the only ones accessible to man, not only fail to touch the depths of his inner life, but give pictures of the tangible world that omit the impressions it evokes which have the deepest meanings.

I am not suggesting that Christian values guided con-

* A. N. Whitehead, *Science and the Modern World*, New York, 1926, pp. 80-82.

duct before modern times, before the "scientific revolution" of the seventeenth century. The epoch of Romanesque and early Gothic architecture and art was undoubtedly a great period for the Christian faith. It was during the eleventh and twelfth centuries that monastic life expanded in Europe as never before or since. In the economic sphere religious constructions then possessed a priority like that claimed today for national defense. It was difficult to deny any expenditure of money and effort, no matter what sacrifices were entailed, for ecclesiastical building and ecclesiastical art. And the only wars for which the Europeans were prepared to make an all-out effort were so-called holy wars against the infidel.

Yet hardly anyone would have claimed then, hardly any historian would claim now, that *temporal* life was carried on according to Christian compassion and love. The age of the Crusades was a time of ghastly physical cruelty and torture, not least on the part of crusaders. The most inhuman punishments were meted out to innocent victims. At home in Europe they were meted out to fellow Europeans and Christians. Tender manners, as Western Europeans and Americans knew them on the eve of two world wars, were mainly an innovation of the seventeenth, eighteenth and nineteenth centuries. They were a mark of the "civilization" which Montesquieu and some of his contemporaries felt to be a creation of the European peoples at home and overseas. This innovation was based largely on a belief in the reality of firm values in connection with faith, art and conduct,* a

* See my *Cultural Foundations of Industrial Civilization*, Cambridge, 1958. Harper Torchbook, 1960.

belief which has been since largely lost. During the past fifty years especially, even humanitarian efforts in social welfare have been accompanied by the disappearance of belief in the universality of the principles which most of our intelligent Christian ancestors accepted. "What is good?" people grew ever fonder of asking, "What is true?"

There is nothing wrong about such questions. It is essential to ask them. This has always been a world of varied conditions for human beings. For instance some are lame and crippled, others healthy, some rich, others poor. Again the same kinds of experiences vary in significance from place to place and from time to time. This has always been a changing world. It is changing now at a dizzy speed in many ways unequaled in the past. Therefore, in the presence of the immense institutions which in our times obscure the individual, what is best, what is right, what is charitable, what is just, what is beautiful, what is compassionate and loving, what is true—are more and more complicated questions, calling for ever more subtle distinctions and thought, and they were never at any period lacking in complications or in subtlety. They *have* to be reconsidered endlessly. The seekers after wisdom, who come closest to being wise, are always asking them. But the seekers after wisdom are endlessly trying to find *answers,* and, in this matter, Pontius Pilate, who asked "what is truth" without waiting for an answer, is no guide. When, as among the generations that have grown up during the twentieth century, such questions become mainly rhetorical, this plays into the hands of the unscrupulous and the cynical.

One of the causes for this recent questioning of spiritual, aesthetic and moral values has been the growing prestige attached to methods of inquiry derived from the natural sciences. Yet it is difficult to see why these values can be effectively discredited by science, if Schrödinger and other scientists are right in finding that the scientific methods, which are so amazingly helpful in some realms, are inappropriate for solving problems in these areas. If science is, as Schrödinger suggests, "ghastly silent" when it comes to questions of the relation of man to God, how can it properly jeopardize the validity of the ultimate purposes which should guide our lives as individuals? The proper approach to questions of faith, beauty and virtue is not by way of the methods used or the discoveries made in the natural sciences. It is through wisdom.

I referred at the outset of these remarks on religion and natural science to the increasingly forbidding and inhuman way in which philosophy and theology have come to be written and taught. It has been frequently suggested during the past twenty years or so, that the great need of our times is for a comprehensive philosophy, for a great philosopher. However that may be, there seems to be a compelling need for a fresh start both in philosophy and in theology. He who speculates philosophically needs to base his speculations much more directly on the real and moving experiences of life. The most hopeful approach would seem to be through those subjects that are "close to our heart." In order to approach truth in that way, the ideas should be based on concrete and intimate experiences in the real world which elude the scientist, and the language used to express them should enchant as well as instruct. Above all it should instruct by enchanting. It is up to the individual, with the help of friends and of the one he loves, if he has the happiness and the pain of being in love, to achieve a philosophical and a religious conception of existence such as will help him to order his life in ways that inspire others. Now more than ever it seems that a conception of life in terms of faith could lead towards truth. Industrialism has plunged us into a world characterized by soulless work and entertainment. The contradictory leadership in philosophical and theological matters offers little help or consolation. It bewilders and repels more often than it clarifies and attracts. Never perhaps in history has it been so vital as now, for those persons who have a genuine thirst for more decent human relations, to maintain open minds and to think through, in a simple, balanced way, the essentials of faith and their significance in the attempt to build a world civilization. The example set by such persons, united if possible in small groups of friends, would not be a substitute for a new philosophy and a new theology, but it might help to give birth to both.

These references to theology in connection with philosophy raise a question which troubles sensitive persons all over the globe: whether it is possible to make faith in God the basic principle in a well-balanced philosophical conception of man. Many doubt it. The impression has spread that faith in God is a superstition, that a religious believer cannot be intelligent, or that, if his intelligence in a scientific realm has been demonstrated, he ceases to be intelligent when he crosses the threshold into religious belief. A friend of mine who had just appointed the new dean of a university divinity school asked me privately for my opinion of this man's inaugural address. I confessed that I had found it difficult to follow, that I had missed any consecutive argument. Whereupon my friend explained: "The dean was trying to say that he believed in God, but he didn't dare!"

The reality of a direct relationship between God and man is an essential part of Christ's message. It provides us with a shield, for which there is no substitute, in seeking to serve not only God but our fellows. It lightens the burdens which such an effort imposes on us. Christ's example makes possible the victory over suffering and misunderstanding and the victory over death which every good human being seeks.

At the same time the shield which faith in a personal relationship with God provides, enables the good human being to concentrate on those aspects of life which lead towards perfection. Stendhal considered the most exalted relationship possible between a man and woman—which he called *amour-passion*—a "miracle" of "civilization." While the highest concept of love has been seldom realized in anything approaching perfection even during modern times, and while it is doubtful if Stendhal understood it for it has to be lived to be understood, it was hardly realized at all before. The concept itself is fundamentally Christian, because it involves the losing of the self in another. This act of personal abnegation, as expressed in Dante's love for Beatrice and in Héloise's love for Abelard, is possible only when love is a personal gift accepted from God. No individual can love another

56

in this way without the faith that love is indestructible. Charity and compassion were first brought fully into the world by the Lord. Through Him the bond which can attach a man to the ones he loves, to his neighbor and even to his enemy, to the extent he is able to follow the example of Christ in loving his enemy, is an eternal bond. Though founded and given its beauty in matter, space and time, love transcends them all because it is part of God Himself.

The supreme moments of exaltation we are granted by this assurance of permanence cannot, of course, be repeated. But the unique beauty that accompanies each of them, and which can unite two persons in an indissoluble union, is made possible by the conviction that love itself in which both participate is undying. That is why the gains we derive from these moments—the sense of participation in God that accompanies them—can never be lost. This faith in the permanence of what is best in us inspires the lives of all those who seek perfection, by building up within them a fund of strength and courage that helps them to resist temptation.

The relation of men and of nature to their Maker is the principal subject of theology. Newman called it "the Science of God, or the truths we know about God put into a system."* If the rise of natural science has led to a weakening of Christian religious belief, this has been contrary to the wishes of many of the greatest scientists. As it developed in early modern times, especially in seventeenth-century England, natural science was some-

* J. H. Cardinal Newman, *The Idea of a University* (London, 1899), p. 61.

times regarded as a most important ally of theology, because it sought to reveal the secrets of the world God had made, a world which as Christians the scientists considered the final testing ground for man. By wresting these secrets from matter, space and time, and from the living bodies of animals and men, the scientists thought they would increase the wonder felt in the presence of the works of God. Observation and experiment, combined with ever more precise quantitative measurements, were to be means of adding to "the truths we know about God."

Scientists ignored a fundamental difference between the objectives of natural science and those of morality. The one aims to show what is, the other what ought to be. The one concerns itself with the finite physical world, the other with the infinite world of the mind and spirit which transcends the matter visible through the most powerful microscopes and telescopes. Unless the objectives of natural science and religion are distinguished and reconciled, and unless both are reconciled with wisdom, the emphasis on science is bound to breed disunity and confusion among the human family, harmful to religion, and in the end to natural science. Such emphasis leads men to see the world too much in material terms, without reflecting upon the divine side of man and the human side of God, through which Our Lord revealed the unique opportunity offered to man to extract from his material experiences that which is lasting.

Science and technology have supplied the ordinary run of men and women not only with means to prolong their lives and to increase their consumption, but also with a vast number of new toys to occupy their leisure time in an age when the need for steady, continuous labor has diminished. Partly as a result of the "misplaced concreteness," which recent university education and research has fostered, human beings, everywhere that scientific knowledge penetrates, are inclined to think of their experiences in terms of the very abstractions which the rise and spread of modern natural science have enthroned.

Let us take an example from the realm of medicine. When a man falls ill he now often learns from his physician about some new virus which is apparently the mischiefmaker. While the physician does not always understand it, it provides him with a convenient subject for talk beside the bed. The patient becomes absorbed in speculating on the way in which this virus develops and moves about within him. His body takes on the aspect of a battlefield, and he envisages with fascination, as a spectator, the reserve forces that he is able to throw against the enemy. When he recovers, the defeated virus provides a fertile topic of conversation. Conversation is an important need of a generation starved for it but left without the materials necessary to make it. How many women's luncheons and tea parties have been saved from silence, if not from boredom, by one guest's talk about her peculiar form of allergy and another's description of her recent bout with diverticultis!

Men and women have come to think of their lives more and more predominantly in pseudo-scientific and pseudo-medical terms. Love, birth and death have been made to seem almost entirely material.

The emphasis on the subjects of scientific inquiry, of

59

technological efficiency, of medicine and surgery, has been accompanied by the notion that, as science and scientific methods alone yield valid positive results, religious dogma should be modified to accord with them. But, if theology has a realm of its own, and if that realm is the unchangeable, how can the truths which belong to this realm, and which men and women dimly perceive, be adjusted to scientific results which are valid mainly for another and different, though related, realm: the realm of positive existence, in which knowledge is continually changing?

Under the influence of false conceptions of the value of scientific knowledge where religion is concerned, many persons who were not committed by their parents to any sect, and·others who withdrew from a church in which they were brought up, reached the conclusion that men are better off without theology and even without any religious belief. Such a conclusion became so prevalent that thousands of the most prominent members of the generation now in early manhood and middle life in the United States, were brought up by their parents and most of their teachers to regard all references to Scripture and to religious matters as evidences of a depravity of the mind from which the enlightened twentieth century was happily to be delivered.

The experience of a scientist's daughter is revealing of a common attitude towards religion in American education and society since the beginning of the present century. This young woman had been continually exposed at home and in school to the new doctrines derived from scientific knowledge by some of the pragmatists. The skepticism of her relatives and teachers frequently involved a denial of the existence of God. There was a learned uncle who even contended that Jesus Christ was a myth, that he had never existed even in human form. So she was indoctrinated with the belief that modern knowledge had proved that the Christian faith is unbelievable.

But unlike so many of her generation, who shared her early experience, she later altered her outlook. In her early twenties she lived in France. There she frequently saw references to Pascal in the writings of eminent men of the time; she heard him extolled as a great mind in debates to which she listened in the Chamber of Deputies. One day, out of curiosity, she bought the then recently published third series of the massive Brunschvicg edition of Pascal's works and began to read some remarkable paragraphs of *Les Pensées*, those where Pascal sets forth with great clarity the difference between the mathematical mind, which can proceed logically from principles that have been artificially created and accepted, and the nimbly discerning mind. As Pascal explains, nimble discernment enables a person to "see the thing at once, in a single glance,"* to grasp intuitively truths concerning the infinitely complicated, delicate relationships of the actual world in which we live, to recognize truths which no logical demonstration can verify, but that are part of the eternity to which man, with God's help, has access. These are the truths of religious faith, of art and of ethics—truths which the

* H. F. Stewart's translation of Pascal's *Pensées*, New York, 1950, pp. 495-97.

61

mathematical mind, by itself, cannot recognize and which it can so easily sterilize.

As a child and adolescent she had acquired a distaste for mathematics. It had always seemed a dry and meaningless subject, irrelevant to anything human. But, to her astonishment, Pascal at once gave it meaning and helped her to understand why it had repelled her. She concluded that the French were right in claiming him as a genius.

Leading the life of continual social activity to which attractive Americans of her class gave themselves up in the 1920's even in France, she found no time to pursue her reading beyond the first twelve pages. But several years afterward an illness offered her an opportunity to revisit the writer who had made such a singularly favorable impression upon her. In the meantime she had acquired the small Massis edition, easier than the heavier Brunschvicg volumes to manage in bed. It opens with *Les Provinciales.* Imagine her surprise, as she began to skim the pages, to find Pascal writing about religious faith with the same assurance, though not quite the same kind of certainty, that characterized his discussion of the nature of the rational processes. Imagine her surprise to find that he treated the tenets of the Christian faith as truths. She discovered too that Christian beliefs, which Pascal discussed, had a relation to the problems of her illness, problems that the doctors who were taking care of her seemed to know nothing about.

She was an intelligent person who had come to trust her own judgment in matters of art and thought. Pascal confronted her with a mind which her experience told her was of the highest order. Her early life in the United States gave her the not erroneous impression that none of her American contemporaries could have distinguished as effectively and clearly as Pascal between the mathematical and the nimbly discerning mind, or have shown so convincingly that it is necessary for a man to employ both in order to arrive at truths in those domains of his concern that are beyond the range of the natural sciences. Was it then possible to be "rational," as Pascal seemed to be, and still have religious faith? Could Pascal be nearer to truths concerning Christian belief than the persons who had brought her up? Was it they, not he, who were prejudiced?

I do not know whether she finally answered these questions, for I lost touch with her. Answers are difficult for the members of her generation and of the one that follows, many of whom in adolescence are even less inclined than she was to believe in the divinity of Christ.

This American story is perhaps of some general interest at a time when so many persons are groping towards a renewal of the Christian faith. Our age prides itself more and more on the practical achievements attributed to its universities and institutes of research. Learned men and their students, however sensitive they may be, seldom have time for an experience like that of this young woman. And while great numbers in the United States and Europe and other places, to which the Christian Gospel was taken centuries ago by priests and pastors, have a religious allegiance at least nominally Christian, the number deeply committed is small. Consequently it is the obstacles to a renewal, and still more to an evolution of faith in the direction of human perfection, which are likely to impress us. The agnostics and the atheists, in what were once considered Christian countries, do not cease to insist that God is dead. Whether we like it or not, they say, the Christian faith will never occupy as important a place again as it did in the evolution of Western civilization. No doubt churches, Christian in origin, can claim hundreds of millions of members. But we are now in the presence of a single world. The number of Christian communicants in Africa represents only a small proportion of the inhabitants. So it is in the Near and Far East, with their enormous populations, exceeding a billion, among whom we find, moreover, other venerable religions. Even in Europe and America, Christianity is mingled with a number of new religions, in which it is often difficult to recognize any Christian content.

In seeking a common basis for understanding, in seeking common purposes for all mankind, should we, as has been suggested, adapt ourselves to all these religions and treat Christianity as simply one among many? Should we mix them all in an enormous goblet? Or should we renounce all religions which involve a belief in the supernatural order of being, and cling only to some version of the religion of humanity adopted more than a century ago by Auguste Comte?

The answer is simple; everything can be adapted to temporal conditions except the truth. If Christ is the Truth, then faith in Him is central to all sides of life and faith is the pivot on which all knowledge should be made to turn. If you have faith, theology is the realm of fixed principles capable of giving meaning and purpose to existence in spite of, indeed because of, rapidly changing material circumstances.

Would an eclipse or even a dilution of Christian faith provide an occasion for rejoicing? Without that faith, we may doubt whether industrial civilization would exist.° The natural sciences, and the technology with which they have come to be allied, cannot occupy the territory which properly belongs to faith.

If Christianity should disappear, it is possible that nothing in the way of final belief will take its place. But unless men are replaced by synthetically manufactured robots, it is more probable that the realm that has been vacated will be occupied by false gods. There is no lack of signs that this occupation has begun.

What is the alternative if we are searching for an ultimate belief which can command assent from men and women everywhere? Is it to make that faith, and the Christian ethics that are part of it, a more living part of temporal existence than ever before? Let us explore this possibility, beginning with another obstacle which seems to stand in its way, the recent efforts to apply scientific methods to those domains where Schrödinger and Hubble suggest they have little or no place.

° See below, especially pp. 104-08.

CHAPTER IV

Religion and Man

EFFORTS TO EXTEND the principles and techniques of the new sciences to the study of man go back at least to the positive philosophy of Auguste Comte, to the mid-nineteenth century. The increasingly astonishing results obtained by modern scientific methods in revealing the nature of the physical and biological universe, led to the treatment of man and of human relations in the abstract ways that were producing such accurate results concerning important aspects of matter, space and time. This treatment provided a great deal of new, interesting and useful knowledge about the behavior of various categories of men and of various societies. It spread the impression that scientific methods have properly almost unlimited scope, that they offer indeed the only sound means of handling human as well as material problems. Consequently scholars in other fields than the sciences and mathematics came more and more to treat men and women, not as individuals, but collectively according to classifications such as their race, their nationality, their profession or occupation, their income, their religious affiliation, etc. In almost every scholarly discipline, some scholars, in accepting the rules and outlook of their specialty, were troubled to find that, notwithstanding the interesting information they were obtaining, they were losing sight of the individual.

A consequence of the efforts to study and analyze men according to categories was to diminish still further the importance attached to personal experiences and private judgments as the basis for decisions on public matters. Another was to render these judgments less sure because they thrive on practice and on confidence in their value. Nevertheless in the realms of faith and of virtue, as of art, the most profoundly engaged workers have persisted in the view that such personal experiences and private judgments furnish the only bases for determining what is true or false, good or bad, beautiful or ugly.

Since there is no way of verifying the deeper truths in the realms of faith or art or morals by observations and measurements, or of demonstrating them mathematically, any approach to certainty in these realms depends upon the power of gifted individuals to discriminate, to recognize the good, to separate the wheat from the chaff. It depends upon the capacity of these and of other individuals, who share their judgments, to make this discrimination count. Faith that in these realms God is the Common Source of guidance, a Source accessible, though dimly and obscurely, to men and women through their inner lives, can be a most precious means of lifting a gifted and disciplined individual to the level of humility and discernment necessary as a foundation for flights of creative intuition.

Scientific inspiration also depends on intuition. It seems perverse, therefore, that the march of modern science, with its insistence on tangible, demonstrable proofs, should have undermined the belief in this Common Source of all truth, simply because there is no experimental or mathematical way of proving the existence of God.

Yet that is what has been happening. It was recognized more than a hundred years ago that it was likely to happen. In the copious diary which the Goncourt brothers kept, we find this interesting entry in 1853. "Gavarni remarked to us: 'Every day science swallows a piece of God. Probably the time will come when our thought processes will be explained in scientific terms as we now explain thunder.' "*

During the hundred years that followed, the older learned subjects, the study of history especially, were invaded by methods of positive verification based on the careful scientific analysis of archeological remains and documents, by attempts to write history in exact quantitative terms. Disciplines less venerable than history—especially political economy—were approached increasingly in terms of statistics and mathematical equations. Scholars in new fields of inquiry such as sociology, psychology, anthropology, psychoanalysis, demography, human ecology, etc., adopted outlooks and methods derived from the natural sciences, especially as these were understood and used in the nineteenth century.

In the course of the past three centuries the old ways of comprehending man and his nature have been almost

* *Journal des Goncourt,* Paris, 1887, I, 47.

completely reversed. How was man once studied? An answer to the question may be found in Father Malebranche's impressive philosophical inquiry, *A Search for Truth*, published in 1674. The book aroused such interest that Malebranche was inundated with letters from all over Europe. Far from offering an example for research into human nature, the natural sciences seemed to Malebranche, as they still did to Schrödinger, to belong in a world which leaves out of account much that is essential to understanding. Malebranche writes that "astronomy, chemistry and almost all other sciences" are "suitable as diversions," but he warns the "honest man" not to be seduced by their glamor into preferring them to "the science of man." On what is that science founded? It is founded precisely on the inner life of the individual, purified from all "false and confused evidence provided by the senses or the imagination," and illuminated by the answers received from God!° For Malebranche the word "science," when used in connection with man, had much the same meaning as two generations earlier for Malherbe, the French court poet, who spoke of "accepting God's will" as the only "science" which gives us peace.

This venerable science of man has now been split into parts, to be swallowed, if not directly by the natural sciences as Gavarni predicted, then by the social and "behavioral" sciences and by a new, inverted "humanism," also clothed in scientific dress. There are scholars who claim that even philosophy, with its ancient value

° Malebranche, *Recherche de la Vérité,* Paris, 1880, vol. i, pp. 23-24.

judgments designed to have universal validity, ought to be abandoned; that, to be legitimate, all research and teaching must be made scientific in the modern exclusive sense of the word, as it is used in the English-speaking countries. In writing recently of *The Rise of Scientific Philosophy,* the late Hans Reichenbach, of the University of California, suggested that ethics in the older sense is unscientific. "The axioms of ethics . . . ," he remarks, "cannot be made cognitive statements at all; there is no interpretation in which they can be called true. When the scientific philosopher denies the possibility of a scientific ethics, he refers to this fact. . . . Even general ethical premises may change with the social environment, and when they are called axioms this term means only that for the content considered they are not questioned."*

Is science to limit the scope of all knowledge? If that limit is imposed, we shall exclude what is to Schrödinger, and to some of the other greatest contemporary scientists, the real world. Can a better race be manufactured in test tubes and by selected breeding after the fashion of horses and dogs, in defiance of that "real world"?

I ask the question because it seems that the march of science beyond its original frontiers, in swallowing God, has not altogether spared man. In the hands of the new specialists, his inner experiences, which cannot be satisfactorily classified and fed to adding machines, become almost valueless. He is more and more diminished to an abstraction, based on the averages of certain things all men and women are supposed to do, for example the

* Los Angeles, 1951, p. 319.

70

quantity of calories or vitamins they consume, the number of cigarettes they smoke, the time they spend before the television set, the candidate they will vote for in the next election. In so far as this course of inquiry is slavishly pursued, the individual becomes something less even than a body, because the body is no longer illuminated by spiritual light. Along with hosts of his fellows he is reduced, in so far as learning is concerned (though sometimes against the will of the learned), to a mathematical symbol, an X, like any scientific datum.

The application of scientific methods to the examination of political, economic and social phenomena during the past century, and especially during the past fifty years, has provided us with a great deal of new knowledge. We have precise information, inaccessible to our ancestors, about the size and the movements of population. We have figures of output, data concerning the incidence of all the principal diseases. A new and far more comprehensive view of historical evolution has been acquired. Accurate information concerning the flow of streams and rivers, the contours of the land, the roads, the sea and air lines is made available through maps and guidebooks. A child can be taught the geographical structure of the planet with an accuracy that would have seemed staggeringly advanced to a Renaissance contemporary of those universal men Erasmus and Michelangelo, both of whom were alive when America was discovered. Now we almost all know just the day we were born, while even the more prominent men of letters and other artists of the generation of Rabelais, who witnessed the Reformation, had only the vaguest idea. They would

71

have been unable to tell their friends when to order a birthday cake or how many candles to stick on it.

With the help of all the new knowledge, men can look at the world, its past and its future, more exactly than ever before. A sensible diet, adequate water drinking, the elimination of cigarette smoking can make for better health in many individuals. Advice by lawyers and investment counselors can help persons to plan their expenditures more rationally. Maps, timetables and travel bureaus can enable them to plan trips more efficiently. Phileas Fogg was a useful pioneer. So, much later, was Charles Lindbergh. In the sphere of sex experience so were Havelock Ellis and later Kinsey.

These vast new perspectives might be used to great human advantage. It is not the existence of fresh data that has led to confusion and to the belittling, sometimes even to the loss, of a rich inner life for men and women. It is the widespread disposition of men to think of the new knowledge as sufficient in itself to bring about progress, or to think that it can be used scientifically to that end, and, even if they do not think so, to conduct their lives as if they did.

An example of the disposition to let social data, gathered scientifically, take the place of life, presents itself in connection with a subject of great importance for happiness—the conditions of successful marriage. One of my older colleagues made a study of those conditions. His qualifications for the task were considered by many as ideal. He had never been married, and so, as a confirmed bachelor, he could be almost perfectly impartial. With the help of research workers paid out of grants from educational foundations, he proceeded to collect masses of material. Carefully examined and interpreted, his data led him to determine at what ages for men and for women, in what professions, etc. marriages had the best chances of lasting. From the point of view of social science, it was a pretty exhaustive inquiry. His conclusions and much of the evidence on which they were based were published. Some of his findings were featured in newspapers.

Information of this kind, of which there are now enormous quantities, has its uses for the individual man and woman, provided they realize how limited is its value in deciding what to do in any particular case; provided, in the case of conjugal relations, they recognize that the endurance of a marriage is not the only test of its success, that the factors "science" is able to isolate with respect even to its endurance are incomplete, and that an important aspect of happiness is left out altogether—the experience of love.

The great question, then, is how the new and illuminating knowledge provided by "scientific" studies of human beings in society can be used for their good. Whether or not it is so used depends, above all, on man himself. Men created science, and the notion, becoming widespread in some circles, that the sciences they have created can be used to take care of men, even to make new men, has its dangers. If men can be manufactured is there any reason to feel confident that the beings produced—by scientists who in their subject matter have to leave out what is "close to our heart"—will have hearts? Is there any reason to suppose these mechanical men, these robots, will have the creative powers of the men who make them? Will they be better fitted to understand each other and develop a world community than the persons they replace, who were born out of what has been hitherto the normal way of conceiving children?

Those mysterious creatures that have peopled the earth, men and women with their minds and hearts and wills moving in most varied ways, have provided the concepts and the motivations which have transformed the external world. It is possible that if men replace themselves by synthetic replicas, our race may abdicate its destiny no less than if the new powers of destruction, also made possible by modern scientific knowledge, are used to put an end to life. So far as I am aware no one has claimed that it is possible to manufacture the soul. And if scientists produce bodies without souls, all that makes life risky and adventurous will disappear, along with all that is eternal. The bodies that replace us might not have in them the quality which for the Christian believer distinguishes us from animals—the power to create new worlds within ourselves. The faith that these creative powers are part of the design of God for man, and an evidence of immortality, is the only guarantee we have that the supreme achievements of men and women transcend the world to which our senses give us direct access. The price of eliminating jealousy and hatred, if that can be done, is likely to be the elimination of compassion and love. The victory over evil and over suffering, which Christ offers men and women, will no longer be possible.

In so far as the social, the behavioral and the human-

istic sciences give the impression that scientifically established facts exhaust the knowledge available to man, in
so far as they suggest that such facts provide the only
basis for decisions, the inner resources of the mind and
the heart, possessed by individuals, are left to rust. In
so far as the mysteries of the soul are denied, a race
could grow up, even if men and women are not manufactured in scientific laboratories, devoid of all sense of
religious, aesthetic and ethical values.

The ravages of human qualities and weaknesses by
the scientific study of man have come at a time when
progress in the natural sciences and in technology has
brought with it a triumph by the machine, and soon also
by automation, in manufacturing, transport and com-
munications. This will leave an ever growing proportion
of workers with only stereotyped tasks. The arrival, by
these means, of what some French professors and men of
affairs call "the scientific society," in which economic
control has shifted to scientists and technical managers,
can have consequences for man which might make him
into a creature very like the one that has come to be the
almost exclusive subject of inquiry in the higher learning. On many fronts, inquiries supported by immense
financial grants are preparing the way for the new synthetic men and women—for the new bundles of atoms
which some biochemists and other scientists are now
being subsidized to help construct.

What, then, if the real road to human understanding
and more peaceful relations is to be found within the
individual and in the fresh inner light which, confronted
with his own possible destruction, he is able to bring to

75

bear upon the great decisions? What if the road is to be found in responses to those problems of God and eternity, beauty and ugliness, virtue and vice, which scientists are wise to leave unanswered if, as Schrödinger suggests, the only answers they are capable of giving are silly answers?

The mistake made because of the scheme of "misplaced concreteness," that has come to dominate the life of our time as led in universities and institutes, is that research and teaching are valued and subsidized only in so far as their sponsors can be plausibly convinced that they will produce tangible results. It is not their existence but their claim to exclusive competence, and the inclusive claims put forward by others on their behalf, that make the social and behavioral scientists and the scientific humanists a danger to the felicity of particular men and women in the difficult world of modern industrialism. These inclusive claims have further diminished the confidence, bordering on certainty, which some of our ancestors possessed in themselves as children of God.

The modern scientific outlook and the approved methods of modern science have encouraged an overemphasis in the temporal world on the changeable and the fleeting to the neglect of the permanent and the essential. In the physical and the biological sciences, new theories and even new statements of laws are continually replacing older ones. As scientific methods have been extended to social and humanistic studies, the view has become general in the social sciences and the humanities that today's knowledge exists mainly to be superseded by tomorrow's; that all constructions of the mind are merely scaffolds for scaffolds, that each generation writes a history, a politics, a sociology or an economics almost entirely irrelevant for the next. In economic science the story of Alfred Marshall's gesture to one of his favorite pupils is suggestive of the viewpoint concerning the study of man that is now frequently accepted almost without question. He presented this pupil with a copy of his classic work, *The Principles of Economics*, the fruit of more than two decades of thought and labor. On the flyleaf he inscribed the young man's name, "in the hope that in due course you will render this treatise obsolete."*

What have been the consequences of the scientific outlook and of modern scientific knowledge for religious faith? What especially have been the consequences for belief in the truth of the Christian Gospel?

The discoveries of the evolutionists, of Darwin in particular, began to make a deep impression in the higher learning before the end of the nineteenth century. These studies were popularly believed to have provided scientific proofs that man is a descendant of the animals, not of Adam as Christians had learned from the Bible. The researches of physiologists, such as Jacques Loeb, went farther in their materialistic interpretations of the human being. According to these researchers man is not only descended from the animals. He is nothing more than an animal. He has no divine element within him. This school was cutting all our bonds with eternity, of which Christ is the witness and the proof. Such scientific claims redoubled the doubts in the learned world

* J. M. Keynes, *Essays in Biography*, London, 1933, pp. 253-54.

concerning the truth of the Gospel. In the light of sub-
sequent scientific studies, the interpretations of Darwin
and later biologists, interpretations which seemed about
to dominate scientific thought at the beginning of the
twentieth century, have now been questioned. Recently
Teilhard de Chardin has re-interpreted our scientific
knowledge of the evolution of the world and of man. He
has sought to reconcile all the scientific work on geology
and evolution with the introduction into the world of a
new species—the human species. Good scientist that he
is acknowledged by competent scientists to have been,
he suggests that man has a direct relation to God possessed by no other form of life.

The work of recent physiologists, notably that of
Charles Sherrington, has also cast doubt on the claims
of those who, like Loeb, thought we could explain
thought fully by analyzing the brain. For Sherrington
man's rationality remains a mystery. For him it is just as
reasonable to suppose, with Aristotle, that the focus of
thought is in the body as to suppose, with Loeb, that it
is in the brain. For Sherrington it is equally impossible to
understand man's inner life in terms of the behavior of
matter whether the intellect is located in the body or in
the brain.

In recent years the all inclusive mechanistic theories
of the nature of man are ceasing to be acceptable to
some of the most distinguished scientists. But this has
hardly impeded the social and behavioral and humanistic scientists from treating men and women as if they
were little more than mechanisms. The "science" of man
has become more inhuman than ever, at any rate in the
Germanic and Anglo-Saxon countries.

Here are examples. I am under the impression that Havelock Ellis, who inaugurated in England at the beginning of the twentieth century scientific studies of sexual behavior, left much more room for the spiritual element in man than did Kinsey in his more recent inquiries into the same subject. I have also the impression that the studies of Durkheim in sociology at the end of the nineteenth century were more philosophical, in the older nonmaterial, nonscientific sense of this word, than those of contemporary American sociologists, just as the present-day statistical studies in political science are less human than those of André Siegfried, who broke new ground in this subject in 1913 with his admirable *Tableau politique de la France de l'Ouest*. In connection with sex if one seeks guidance concerning what Stendhal called *amour passion,* one will be little helped by either Ellis or Kinsey. This passion cannot be understood in terms of animal instincts or of any logical process of reasoning. More illumination is often provided by reading books such as *Tom Jones* and *Manon Lescaut,* literary masterpieces of an earlier age, of the age when the word "civilization" was introduced into language. The power of love described in those eighteenth-century novels is derived from its Christian origin. Animal that he is, man is shown, by virtue of God's gifts and God's grace, to have sometimes the power to guide his body (imperfectly of course) according to the divine will and to love another person as if that person were himself. A book like *Tom Jones* was an expression of an immense Christian effort, that had been deepened at the time of the Wars of Religion, to reconcile temporal life with heaven. The initiative had come from a few persons born in the late fifteenth century. Among them were Erasmus and Titian and Rabelais. I am thinking of Erasmus' exposure of monastic life, Titian's painting reconciling sacred with profane love, Rabelais' Abbaie de Thèleme, to which women and men were admitted with the motto over the entrance to "do as they pleased."

Has the development of the social sciences really rendered the New Testament obsolete? Have we scientific evidence that the new law of universal love presented in the Gospel is invalid? Has science proved that God is not united with man through Christ and that man has consequently no existence, by virtue of his soul, independent of worldly and material conditions? Has he no power to transform worldly and material conditions in the image not of what is but of what ought to be, as that image is presented in the Gospel?

These questions cannot be resolved in a few paragraphs. Yet it may be suggested that the findings of sociology and all the new sciences, including the theories of evolution put forward by Darwin, have brought no conclusive proofs against the truth of the Gospel. The studies of primitive peoples, by such scholars as Sumner and Westermarck, have revealed a great variety of manners, customs and religious beliefs among the peoples of the past and present. But there is really nothing new in this. Herodotus had written about a similar diversity 2500 years ago. It was common knowledge among the Greek philosophers of Herodotus' time. Yet the prestige of Greek philosophy, and the discussions of relativism among the cultured Athenians and their Roman followers throughout the Mediterranean basin, did not

treated as a simple matter of accidental preference. Moral values should not be a diversion, but the heart of every subject of religious inquiry. We can conceive of a future science of man only in so far as we are able to outgrow and transcend the prejudices and the methods of what Whitehead felicitously called "misplaced concreteness" derived from modern science. It is real concreteness we should seek. It is individual men and women as wholes (not as split up by the specialist or as reduced to atoms by the scientist) who must conduct the inquiries and decide what shall be their objectives. These decisions should be made less in the light of what Pascal called "the mathematical," than of what he called "the nimbly discerning" mind. It is the intuitive understanding of a few wise men, who combine the conscience with the heart, with deep experience and with wide knowledge of the recent achievements in science and technology, that might help us to confront the reality which has been lost sight of in the unreal world created by scientific research of every kind. If these men are able to transcend the so-called "scientific" methods, to make scientific knowledge the servant rather than the master of their thought, the free mind might achieve a place in the life of our time that it has never had before. Ways different from those that have prevailed might be discovered to utilize the knowledge provided by the study of archeology, sociology, anthropology, etc. Liberated from "misplaced concreteness," a few exceptionally gifted and dedicated men could employ the facts obtained from research in history, economics, politics, archeology, sociology and anthropology, to construct en-

during works of the mind. We might then look forward
to interpretations of scientific knowledge guided by a
hierarchy of artistic and ethical values derived from
direct experience with life.

If we possess a spiritual, artistic and moral hierarchy
of values, based on faith and love, what is likely to strike
us in looking at religion is less the diversity of religious
sects than the universality of religious feeling in all societies. This leads us to think that our nature cannot
subsist without spiritual nourishment transcending the
visible world, that spiritual nourishment is a universal
need. In so far as history is a guide, it seems impossible
for a sensitive person to live without faith.

Man is born not to serve himself but "to love his neighbor." This was the counsel that the greatest surgeon of
the sixteenth century prefixed to his treatise on surgery.
Shall we say that this advice was simply a matter of Am-
broise Paré's personal bias? Shall we say he was indulging in propaganda? Paré managed to cover his tracks so
well that no historian (and few of his contemporaries)
has been able to determine for certain whether he was a
Huguenot or a Catholic. He concealed his religion for
reasons of safety in an age of religious warfare. His admonition could not betray him, for it is no monopoly of
Catholicism or Protestantism. It transcends both. Freud
has taught us that it is older than Christianity.* It may
well have existed potentially as an ultimate hope from
the time that human life was introduced into the world.
But it was Christ who first asked us to love our *enemies*.

* Cf. Sigmund Freud, *Civilization and Its Discontents* (New York,
1930), p. 81.

And it is in and through Him that we can be guided by divine love in our relations with our kind.*

When we consider, not the Gospel, but the history of Christianity, we are led to the conclusion that its significance cannot be dismissed as a mere matter of the mores of a particular tribe, race, nation or society. Christianity was born among the Jews in Palestine almost two thousand years ago. It established itself in the Roman Empire as part of the classical society of the Mediterranean area. Yet the divinity of the New Law consisted not in the persons who adopted it but in the offer it conveyed to every human being on earth. Beside that universal gift of Christ, all other religions are tribal. No classical tradition grew in strength with the decline of the Roman Empire except the rising Christian tradition. Men ceased to read even commentaries upon the commentaries on the works of Aristotle and the other great writers of antiquity. But their faith deepened during the Dark Ages when economic life became more primitive, as they repeated the plain chant in unison and listened to the Gospel as recited by the priests. Faith was hardly weakened by the break between the Western and the Eastern church. With the rise of European society and the growing strength of the papacy in the eleventh and twelfth centuries, the Christian Gospel assumed a universality in the life of the Western peoples, and also in that of the very different Eastern peoples of the Balkans

* On the contributions of Christianity to civilization, see Alexis de Tocqueville, *Oeuvres Complètes,* vol. ix, Paris, 1959, pp. 45-46, 57-58 (Tocqueville to Gobineau). These letters of Tocqueville's, which I read after this essay of mine had been written, show to what a point I share his views concerning the contribution of the Christian faith to the coming of modern civilization.

and of Russia, that it never possessed among the classical peoples into whose world it was introduced. The
Christian faith, derived partly from the ancient Hebrew
religion, has provided consolation to a medley of races,
living under a great diversity of economic and political
systems, and belonging to an almost equally numerous
diversity of cultures. An ethical study of sociology and
of all the subject matter of the social sciences is capable
of raising doubts in the minds of intelligent men concerning the widely popularized view that faith in the
Lord is a superstition.

If the word "intelligence" is reserved, as it has tended
to be increasingly during the past century, to facts and
theories whose validity can be established by positive
science, do we not deprive men, if they wish to remain
"intelligent," of exploring a realm which is no less real
than the realms to which scientific investigations admit
us? If we compare the truths revealed by science with
those revealed by the Christian faith, are the fundamental religious beliefs of Christianity any more fantastic than the scientific beliefs which are now accepted
widely as perfectly rational? Established concepts in the
natural sciences are sometimes no less contrary to our
experiences than the belief that God became a man.
About a schoolteacher who invokes modern science to
keep his pupils from going to mass, Simone Weil says
justly: "In so far as this teacher's capacity of verification
is concerned, the theory of Einstein is at least as little
founded and at least as contrary to common sense as the
Christian tradition concerning the immaculate conception and the virgin birth."*

* *L'Enracinement,* p. 203.

The sciences employed during the past hundred years in the study of man have produced no solid proof that what appears fantastic and improbable is necessarily less true in connection with the inner lives of human beings than in connection with nature as it has been explored by generally accepted scientific methods. The abundant and often precise information, the theories, concerning the behavior of men in societies, obtained by the social and the humanistic sciences, may prove most useful for the "science of man himself," in the older sense in which Malebranche used the phrase. But the ways in which the social and humanistic sciences have formulated problems, and the methods they have employed in dealing with these problems, give little help to the individual who, in his inner life, is trying to find the light without which he is lost. They often confuse him and get in the way of his search for that light. The subject that needs to be explored is not man as an abstraction or as a body without a soul. It is man as a person in the presence of eternal values, which become meaningful only with the help of faith. The truths about human beings need to be sought by means other than those which the social and humanistic have borrowed from the natural sciences. That is why the individual who welcomes the light offered by God is essential to the search for civilization. Faith is the only slavery which can deliver a man from slavery.

One reason that none of the modern sciences has recognized how essential is faith, not only to salvation but to happiness, is found in the fact that, partly perhaps because of the fragmentation of knowledge, men have expected from religion direct results of a material kind. A striking example is afforded by the recent tendency to judge Christian churches, Christian dogmas and even Christ Himself, according to their contributions to economic prosperity.

CHAPTER V

Religion and Wealth

So far this inquiry into the Christian faith has centered around the doubts cast on the truth of the Gospel by the conceptions of truth which have come to prevail in the life of our times. In as far as possible I have considered the tenets of the faith independently of the Roman Catholic Church, with its numerous ecclesiastical foundations, and the other churches, Catholic and Protestant, founded to represent Christ.

Such a handling of the subject resembles less the play without Hamlet than Hamlet without the play. When our concern is with the purpose of existence, it is not perhaps unnatural to consider Christ's words and His presence as infinitely more important than the clergy and the institutions, with their rules, which clergymen have organized, promulgated and administered. Nevertheless religious institutions and the men or women who direct them have always taken a powerful part in the preservation and the spread of the Christian faith. They have interpreted it for the laity. It is ecclesiastics who have conceived, formulated and administered the regulations intended to govern communicants. When we seek to learn lessons from history, it is difficult to separate the role of religious faith from ecclesiastical history.

In treating the historical influence of religion, it has long been common to concentrate on the effects of interpretations of the Gospel by orthodox theologians and on the rules and the governments of particular churches. In recent times, with the growing emphasis on the material sides of life, some historical students have set about to determine the influence of church dogma and authority on wealth. During the nineteenth century, with the spread of specialization and the rising prestige of scientific methods beyond the natural sciences, a new species of historian was born: the economic historian. Economic historians have been concerned from the outset with economic progress, and more recently, under the spell of quantitative scientific methods, progress has been made almost synonymous with economic growth. I know whereof I speak because I was perhaps one of the first sinners in this respect, as also in the application of the comparative method as a means of establishing relative rates of economic growth in various countries and regions and at different times.* What conclusions have historical authorities reached, as a result of new knowledge concerning material development, about the relations between religion, as expressed and interpreted and

* Cf. John Nef, *The Rise of the British Coal Industry*, London, 1932, Part I, chap. iii; "A Comparison of the Industrial Growth in France and England from 1540 to 1640," *Journal of Political Economy*, XLIV (1936); A. P. Usher, "Two Notable Contributions to Economic History," *Quarterly Journal of Economics*, Cambridge, Mass., Nov. 1933, pp. 171-80.

administered by ecclesiastics, and the increase in wealth?

With the study of economic history in the twentieth century the impression became prevalent that the Roman Church had been an obstacle to growth and so to progress. The idea was actually much older than the systematic study of economic history. More than two centuries ago Josiah Tucker, a busy Anglican dean of whom it was said that religion was his trade and trade his religion, sought to reconcile the doctrines of political economy with the teachings of his Church. He made comparisons (for there is nothing strictly new about the comparative method in history either) between the economic opportunities offered the enterprising businessman in Roman Catholic France and in Protestant England. Among the disadvantages for the French, which Tucker enumerated, was "the Romish Religion, which has added to its other Absurdities, a Spirit of Cruelty and Persecution, so repugnant to the Scope and Tendency of the Gospel."* Long after Tucker's time, and when his contribution had been largely forgotten, this thesis was amplified. Between 1895 and 1905 two essays by precursors of the later so-called "social scientists" altered Tucker's argument, while supporting his view that the Catholic Church had stood in the way of economic progress. The first was by Sir William Ashley, the second by Max Weber. Both dealt with the influence of the Reformation on capitalistic enterprise. Ashley laid em-

---

* Josiah Tucker, *A Brief Essay on the Advantages and Disadvantages Which Respectively Attend France and Great Britain with Regard to Trade*, 2nd ed. London, 1950, p. 24.

phasis on the religious attitude towards interest taking; Weber on the religious attitude towards diligence in all economic activities. Ashley suggested that the Protestant Churches, especially those descended from Calvin, removed obstacles to the pursuit of private profit in business; Weber suggested that Protestant ethic provided private enterprise with positive stimuli. Weber's essay, which was given in Germany as a course of lectures, has gained wide fame, especially in the United States, among professors and students in the universities, until it is sometimes taken almost for granted that the doctrines of Calvin were basic in forming the "capitalist spirit," and so in stimulating economic growth and the coming of industrialism.

Professor Tawney, in his *Religion and the Rise of Capitalism,* a much more eloquent exposition of the subject than Weber's published lectures, introduced certain qualifications to Weber's conclusions, but did not alter the main argument that the dogma of the Catholic Church had served as a kind of brake on the coming of "capitalism," a brake which the spread of Calvinism did much to release. Perhaps the most dedicated and authentic English socialist of his generation, Tawney is not a good Marxist historian and he is, to a degree that has been rare among Anglo-Saxon economic historians, a sincere practicing member of the Anglican Church, for whom the belief that God became a man is by no means fantastic. Therefore for him the justification for the Christian faith could not be found in its contribution to capitalism, in which he saw principally the weaknesses and casuistries. What emerges both from his book and

91

from Weber's essay is that, in modern times, the Roman Church, and in the beginning the Anglican Church as well, by the religious doctrines they supported, were less favorable to capital accumulation and to business practices leading to large profits, than the Protestant Churches, especially those which adopted Calvinistic theology and worship.

It is a novel idea, which Tawney did not share, that a Christian church has any obligation to multiply material riches. If a man believes in the truth of the Gospel, the question that preoccupies him is which church serves Christ best, and it is difficult to regard that as exclusively (or even primarily) an economic question. Nevertheless a high material standard of living, such as is being achieved in many countries under industrialism, and the attainment of a decent standard everywhere, have tremendous importance for welfare in the crowded world of the twentieth century. The starvation of tens of millions of people is a staggering blow to the efforts of men to achieve civilization. No true follower of Christ can envisage without profound dismay the increase or even the continuance of misery. Without losing sight of the fact that the ultimate purpose of the Christian faith is the spiritual salvation of individual men and women, it is proper to consider how far a strong church, and in particular the Roman Catholic Church, has actually interfered with economic progress.

The controversy initiated by Ashley and Weber does not seem to me to have settled at all satisfactorily the question of the Christian contribution to the triumph of industrialism. To leave the subject with the notion that the Reformation and the spread of Calvinist worship were the principal religious contributions to wealth does not give a true historical view of the relation of the Founder to the material success achieved in modern times.*

If one does not simply go over the ground already laboriously tilled by followers and critics of Weber or Tawney, but looks at the question afresh, it appears as an immensely complicated one. For instance the influence of the Roman Church has varied at different times. During the period from the early eleventh through the thirteenth century the Church added greatly to its wealth and power. This was also a period of growing population in Europe and of rapidly increasing agricultural and industrial production, a period of striking commercial prosperity in many towns and villages. The standard of living apparently rose in most regions for most classes of the population, including the peasants. In fact there is hardly an age of equal duration, until the eighteenth or even the nineteenth century, during which Europeans generally prospered so much as in this medieval period, sometimes called the age of faith.

The economic prosperity and growth in the times of the Crusades were accompanied by a more than proportionate increase in the economic influence of the Roman

---

* I have treated the subject of the Reformation and what has been called "the rise of capitalism" somewhat more fully in "La Riforma Protestante e l'origine della civiltà industriale," *Economia e Storia,* ii, 1955, pp. 18 ff. And I am at work on a long book in which I hope to consider the contributions of the Christian faith, from its beginnings in the first century, to the origins, the birth and the triumph of industrial civilization.

Church. Cathedrals, churches and monasteries, built during the eleventh, twelfth and thirteenth centuries, cost a sum equivalent to a great many billions of dollars in terms of present-day American money, at a time when the yearly dividend of all the countries of Western Europe ran into only hundreds of millions instead of hundreds of billions. Some recent economists have held that there are conditions which render a program of public works beneficial to economic welfare, even though the works themselves are of no practical use for the production or the carriage of commodities. May this not have been the case when the Roman Church, through its multiplying ecclesiastical foundations, became the principal employer of labor in Europe?

Religion was then an integral part of life to an extent that it is difficult for us today to imagine. A great number of persons throughout Western Christendom were filled with an enthusiasm for religious building and for religious art to adorn the churches and even the monasteries. The orders given by the multiplying ecclesiastical foundations for construction work of many kinds and especially for works of beauty dedicated to God, the participation of many monks in the labor of building and decoration, provided a remarkable stimulus to economic effort in general, long before economic effort began to take a form resembling mass production.

Scholars who are influenced by impressions derived from the controversy over religion and capitalism, as developed especially by Ashley and Weber, might ask whether economic progress, as measured statistically, would not have been more rapid from the eleventh through the thirteenth century without the Church, or if the Reformation and Calvinism had appeared much earlier, for instance at the beginning of the twelfth century. This is a futile, unrealistic issue to raise. The historian is not a chemist. He cannot experiment with societies as a scientist often can with the substances he handles. He cannot leave aside one of the major elements in the history of a period—in this case the Roman Catholic Church—and find out what would have happened if there had been no such thing. He deals with human beings and the institutions they establish. Given the facts of medieval economic development, as these are coming to be known, the burden of proof is on those who claim that the Roman Church was an obstacle to economic growth from *c.* 1000 to *c.* 1300.[1] At that time ecclesiastical enterprise was making important novel contributions to production, not only through its orders for workers but through its initiative in connection with crude machinery. With the conditions of material progress that prevailed during this epoch, it is doubtful whether a weakening of ecclesiastical power and a diminution of ecclesiastical wealth would have proved a stimulus.[2]

Later, at the end of the Middle Ages, the conditions of economic progress changed, together with the place of the Church in civilized life. In the twelfth and even the thirteenth century, mining and metallurgy could still be undertaken effectively in most of the mining districts of

[1] John Nef, "L'Art religieux et le progrès économique au moyen age," *Association pour L'Histoire de la Civilisation,* Toulouse, 1952-53, pp. 23-29.

[2] Compare above, p. 52.

Europe by small partnerships of manual workers. But after the thirteenth century further progress in many mining districts came to require much more costly investments. These were hardly forthcoming in any considerable quantity until two hundred years afterwards. By that time, which is to say by the late fifteenth century, the need for large capital investments was felt in a number of other industries where small-scale enterprise had been the rule in the thirteenth century. Meanwhile the prestige and the influence of the papacy had shrunk, and along with it that of a great number of subsidiary ecclesiastical foundations. In the economic realm, these foundations had become, generally speaking, less enterprising than before. The religious and also the lay clergy, who had often taken a direct part in religious building from the eleventh until the early fourteenth century, were less disposed to do so. In the building industries, the place of ecclesiastics in economic innovations was coming to be filled by the increasingly powerful sovereign political authorities—national states, principalities and growing towns—and by rich private merchants, of whom Jakob Fugger is the most celebrated.

On the eve of the Reformation the Church, through its ecclesiastical foundations, still had titles to about as much property as in the thirteenth century. But, with the changes in the authority and the initiative of the clergy, their wealth exercised something of a brake on the kinds of economic progress which brought about the eventual triumph of industrial civilization. Ecclesiastics were not ready to invest large sums in business enterprises within their own lands. They were seldom willing to lease these lands on as favorable terms as lay landlords to others—

principally town merchants—who wanted to venture large sums. And land that belonged to the Church, unlike land in the hands of laymen, could rarely be bought. So the most enterprising industrial adventurers were at a disadvantage when they sought to exploit mineral wealth or other resources that remained in the possession of ecclesiastical foundations.

It is perhaps here that the Reformation contributed most directly and immediately to the investment of large blocks of capital in the exploitation of the baser ores and minerals, where success depended on liberal mining and metallurgical concessions. In sixteenth-century England, the dissolution of the monasteries led to the transfer of a substantial portion of all the lands that were rich in mineral wealth from the Church to the Crown and to laymen. Something like an "early industrial revolution" took place in Great Britain during the reigns of Elizabeth I, James I and Charles I, which is to say from about 1560 to 1640. It was based to a large extent on the exploitation of coal resources, many of which passed out of ecclesiastical hands, partly as a result of the Reformation. It is indeed probable that, by reducing the wealth and economic influence of the clergy, the Reformation contributed not only to the progress of coal mining but of metallurgy, and also of the rapidly increasing number of manufactures whose sponsors found it profitable to turn from wood or charcoal to coal-burning forges, furnaces and ovens. As a consequence, new technical problems were raised in an acute form at the juncture of the sixteenth and seventeenth centuries by the expansion of the coal industry: the need for more powerful drainage engines, for railways with horse-drawn wagons to carry coal overland, and for new methods of smelting which would make it easy and cheap to convert ores to metals with coal fuel. It was the solution of these problems towards the close of the eighteenth century that precipitated the industrial revolution in Great Britain. So, by facilitating the expansion of the British coal industry, the weakening of the power of the Roman Church in sixteenth-century Britain was a factor that encouraged the coming of modern industrial society.

In France and most continental countries, no such wholesale transfer of property from ecclesiastical to private ownership took place during the sixteenth and seventeenth centuries. The Church retained its landed wealth until the French Revolution. Statistics assembled on the eve of it, concerning the ironworks in many provinces, suggest that the larger, more efficient enterprises were almost invariably in the lands of laymen rather than of ecclesiastical foundations.[1] The conservative attitude on the part of the clergy to the economic development of landed property was not special to the Roman Church. The Anglican influence was much the same. At the beginning of the eighteenth century Daniel Defoe explained the backwardness of building near Wolverhampton on the ground that "the land, for the chief Part, being the Property of the Church . . . the Tenure [is] not such as to encourage People to lay out their money upon it."[2] In so far as religious history is concerned, what

[1] H. and G. Bourgin, *L'Industrie sidérurgique en France,* Paris, 1920. And see the figures derived from this book in John Nef, *The United States and Civilization,* Chicago, 1942, pp. 158-59.

[2] Daniel Defoe, *A Tour Through the Whole Island of Great Britain,* 1769 ed., vol. ii, p. 411.

made Great Britain more susceptible to economic growth than France during a hundred years following the Reformation was less the "Absurdities" of "the Romish Religion," of which Tucker wrote, than the diminution in ecclesiastical wealth in England, Scotland and Wales.

The conservative influence of churchmen in Europe towards economic development during modern times is partly explained by the fact that ecclesiastics did not adjust themselves readily to the kinds of production and consumption that led in the direction of modern industrial society. Monks and priests found it normal to employ their time, and to invest the capital of their orders or spend the income they controlled, in other ways than by installing new machinery or by purchasing manufactured products that were cheap and plentiful. In 1676 Sir William Petty, one of the fathers of economic thought, was so strongly of the opinion that a large clergy was a handicap to the kind of economic progress that had already caught the imagination of Englishmen, that he passed on an exaggeration which we read with a little surprise, coming as it does from so meticulous a statistician. "The Hollanders," he wrote, "observe that in France and Spain . . . the Churchmen are about one hundred for one, to what they use or need; the principal care of whom is to preserve Uniformity, and this they take to be a superfluous charge.* After the mid-sixteenth century neither the Dutch nor the English had suffered from this charge as much as the French, the Italians and the Spaniards. This partly accounts no doubt for the

* *The Economic Writings of Sir William Petty*, ed. by C. H. Hull, Cambridge, 1899, vol. i, p. 263.

more rapid growth in the volume of output in seven-teenth-century Holland and Great Britain. The ritual of the Roman, and also of the Anglican Church, called for expenditures on works of art to be contemplated, more than on the multiplication of cheaper objects for daily use. These works of art made a contribution of their own to the eventual triumph of industrialism, but the fash-ioning of them did not stimulate the labor-saving inven-tions of the eighteenth-century.

The diminution of ecclesiastical property and the shrinkage in the size of the clergy were not the only ways in which the Reformation seems to have furthered eco-nomic growth. According to Weber, and others who have amplified his argument, Calvinism, particularly as it was developed in the religious sects which represented it after the mid-seventeenth century, provided a stimu-lus that was lacking under other forms of the Christian faith. It seems to me that Weber and Tawney were right in thinking that Calvinism became, in a number of ways, more favorable to the rise of industrialism than Catholi-cism. Whether the successful businessman as an indivi-dual was spurred on to greater efforts, as Weber sug-gested, by an assurance that success meant he would find himself among the elect at the Day of Judgment, is per-haps debatable. However that may be, Calvinistic wor-ship was certainly austere; it left the problems of salva-tion to the individual without priestly help. Therefore it reduced greatly the time and money wanted for the cultivation of religious art and for the maintenance of clergymen. In these ways faithful Calvinists were left much freer than faithful Catholics to devote their energies to economic improvements leading to steam power, railways and cheap iron—improvements which did not fit readily into the ancient pattern of industrial enterprise as it had formerly been carried on almost everywhere.

What a study of the last four centuries of history leads us to question is not the Weber thesis itself, but the disproportionate importance that has been given to it as an explanation of the industrialized world in which we live. It is unlikely that in this respect Weber would be a good Weberite if he were alive today, any more than Marx would be a good Marxist. The economic individualism, stimulating to modern economic progress, had many sources. The origins of the industrialized world in men's minds became compelling, at the end of the sixteenth and in the early seventeenth century, through the scientific revolution and the new technological problems that were raised independently of it at much the same time. The changes during these years in the directions taken by thought concerning the nature of truth, and the roads to its discovery, were by no means confined to the Protestant countries of Europe. So the efforts that have been made to claim that these changes were to an important degree brought about by Calvinism are unconvincing.

It was not merely the introduction of new methods of scientific inquiry and the new importance given to particular technological problems, raised notably by the coal industry, that eventually precipitated the industrial revolutions of the past century and a half. For the full exploitation of the possibilities of modern science and technology, a confidence in the capacity of human beings to use new knowledge for good was necessary. There had to be a fresh belief in man. Whence did it come? Did it come, as some nineteenth-century writers suppose (Buckle among them), from a break with Christianity, a break away from what these men regarded as the superstitious dogmas of the Christian faith? That seems to be too simple an explanation.

Let us consider the indirect influences of Christian history in bringing a new confidence to man. Here is an important aspect of the relation between religion and wealth, which the controversy over the question has neglected hitherto.

It is pretty generally believed that, in recent times, the rapid industrialization of the planet has depended upon the application of scientific discoveries, made possible by new scientific methods, to practical technological problems. The new methods began to be extensively used, and the urgent new technological problems intensively raised, in the late sixteenth and early seventeenth centuries. But it was some time after that before we find much effective collaboration between scientists and what we should now call engineers. It was apparently not until the early eighteenth century that a serious beginning was made in this direction. In 1722 the famous French scientist, Réaumur, "combined in a metallurgical work the viewpoint of the pure scientist with an interest in what had been, and what could be, achieved in practice."* Not long afterwards, in 1742, a much less well-remembered scientist—an Englishman named Benjamin

---

* Cyril Stanley Smith, *Réaumur's Memoirs on Steel and Iron*, Chicago, 1956, pp. xx, xxii.

Robins—applied to actual results in the field, almost for the first time, scientific theories concerning the course followed by balls shot out of cannon and concerning the composition of gunpowder.[1] Yet even after that the eagerness to make new scientific discoveries useful had little or nothing to do with the inventions of Watt and Cort, which seem to have been of decisive importance in stimulating the sharp rise in the rate of economic growth in England during the seventeen-eighties, when the industrial revolution really began.[2] Both of these men, and almost all the famous inventors of the eighteenth century, worked empirically at practical problems without much scientific knowledge and without much help from scientists. Not until the nineteenth and above all the twentieth century were the possibilities inherent in modern scientific discoveries generally and sensationally realized in industry, transport and communication.

Why was there such a long lag between "the scientific revolution" and the industrial revolutions that have brought the triumph of industrialism? One of the reasons was the reluctance of scientists to have their solutions put to practical use. Until after the discoveries of Newton, who apparently shared this reluctance, they felt a compunction, which seems to have prevailed in earlier times, and which was demonstrated in Archimedes' famous refusal to disclose the weapons with which he defended Syracuse against the Romans, to conceal fresh

[1] See John Nef, *War and Human Progress*, Cambridge (Mass.), 1950, pp. 194-95.

[2] *Ibid.*, chap. xv; John Nef, "Coal Mining and Utilization," *A History of Technology*, ed. Charles Singer et al., Oxford, 1957, vol. iii, pp. 72 sqq.

103

knowledge lest it be used for destructive purposes. Scientists seem to have felt strongly an obligation to defend mankind from the evil which lurks in human nature. As late as Newton's time, they never worked, as they have come now frequently to do, in teams; publicity was in its infancy; there were no newspaper and radio programs to proclaim sensational scientific discoveries. So effective concealment was sometimes possible.

During the eighteenth century, as is shown by Benjamin Robins' treatise called *New Principles of Gunnery*, the hesitation felt by previous scientists to disclose their results was disappearing. In still more recent times there grew up a naive confidence in human nature, which led many modern scientists to disregard caution altogether. Their optimism reminds me of an historical colleague of mine, who, in the presence of some thirty scholars, whom he knew only slightly, and whose discretion he had no particular reason to trust, purveyed what he thought was secret knowledge concerning Abraham Lincoln's diseases, after cautioning his listeners not to tell anyone else what he was telling them! Here was an amusing reversal of the age-old precept that the only sure way to keep a secret is to confide it to no one.

Hope in the discretion and the goodness of man arose partly out of a growing belief that the new powers men were finding to wrest from nature secrets concerning the physical and biological universe—to advance, with the new methods, knowledge of astronomy, physics, chemistry, physiology and metallurgy—were indicative of a higher level of development than had existed before on this planet. Voltaire, Montesquieu, Burke and Gibbon, for

among them François de Sales and Vincent de Paul—
was that purgatory is right here in the world. Therefore
the religious counselor has a supreme opportunity, by
acting as the representative of Christ, to exercise Christian virtue in helping those in all classes of the population
who suffer. The movement that followed to create a true
Christian laity was by no means entirely Roman Catholic
in origin. As Bishop of Geneva, François de Sales is said
to have had in his possession sixty-three heretical books.
Among them was a pioneering Protestant work by a
French Huguenot, Jean de Lespine, *Excellent Discours
sur le repos et le contentement de l'esprit.* Lespine at-
tacked all the older philosophies and systems of ethics,
for having failed to recognize the real remedies offered
by the Gospel, and for having failed to base morality on
faith in the perfectibility of man. Much of François de
Sales' teaching and action, as we look back, seems to aim
at the realization in the world of the precepts of this
Protestant work. He and his female comrade, Jeanne de
Chantal, and Vincent de Paul strove, as none of their ecclesiastical predecessors had done, to bring charity and
compassion to the ordinary man and woman, to express
for them the understanding love that we find Christ
spreading in the Gospel. They founded orders outside
the cloister, not confined by vows of poverty or even of
permanent chastity, but enlisting the richest and most
aristocratic elements in European society. These priestly,
saintly men and women joined and complemented the
work of artists such as Poussin, Racine and Molière, of
mistresses of social perfection such as Madame de Ram-
bouillet, Madame de Lafayette and Madame de Sévigné,

of theological historians such as Bossuet and Fénélon, of philosopher-mathematicians such as Descartes and Pascal. A hope that was new and that was derived from the Renaissance—from the attempts to reconcile the sacred and profane[1]—was taken seriously for the first time. It was a hope in the power of men and women working in society to order their relations—individual and social—so as to maintain at least a minimum of decency.

To many Europeans the age of Louis XIV seemed to offer a partial, if imperfect, fulfillment of the promise contained in the lives and the work of these innovators. In the times of Louis XV, Montesquieu linked the improvements in the treatment of human beings by their fellows to the coming of commerce, which was providing, to some extent, a humane alternative to total war. As he put it in De l'Esprit des lois, "Wherever there is commerce, there are tender manners, and wherever there are tender manners there is commerce."

The rise of civilization was accompanied, then, by novel improvements in the ways men treated their neighbors. It was also accompanied by the discovery of woman and of the spiritual strength she possesses as an individual.[2] It was her tenderness, her natural disposition to be loving, that caught men's imagination. The emergence of civilization, to which gentle manners contributed, engendered the hope and sometimes the conviction, that the intelligence, the rational faculties, were getting the upper hand over man's violent propensities.

[1] See above, pp. 79-80.

[2] John Nef, *Cultural Foundations of Industrial Civilization*, Cambridge, 1958, pp. 103-06.

107

As a result scholars in all sectors, especially the natural sciences, bathed in the novel assurance that worldly relations were improving and would continue indefinitely to improve. Worry diminished over the dangers in probing the secrets of the material world and spreading the knowledge thus obtained. This contributed to the sensational economic progress of the nineteenth century.

The attempts to realize the Christian ethics after the Reformation and the Counter Reformation seem to have been at the roots of the new confidence men and women were coming to feel in their neighbors and themselves. The fresh hope in human nature was Christian in origin; it was fostered within the Christian churches, and not least within the Roman Catholic Church, by a few innovators with profound convictions that Christ can help the individual in his inner life, and so create better men and women and better societies than have ever existed before. This indirect religious contribution to the extraordinary economic wealth of modern times perhaps more than offset any direct handicaps imposed by the Christian religion and the Christian churches upon the triumph of industrialism. It was perhaps less the decline of clerical control over our lives, than the new spiritual hopes infused into them, that provided the stimulus for the phenomenal economic progress in modern times.

The assumption that underlies most of the discussion of religion and capitalism since the times of Dean Tucker, two centuries ago, would seem odd to the early Christian fathers or to medieval theologians like Anselm or Thomas Aquinas. The assumption is that a church

must somehow justify its existence by the contribution
that it makes to material progress. That is hardly the purpose of which Christ speaks in the Gospel when what He
says seems to foreshadow a Church founded in His
name. The purpose is salvation through the personal
inner lives of individuals, and the role of material
worldly riches in salvation is always, to say the least, subsidiary to the riches of the spirit, to compassion and love
even more than to justice. For the individual, material
wealth is often represented as more of a handicap than
an advantage. While it would be unchristian to suggest
that a Christian church should stand in the way of *social*
justice, it is not collective but individual welfare, and
welfare in the deepest spiritual sense, that is the primary
object for which a Christian church exists. It is easy to
lose sight of this objective, for the vast organizations of
our times, including the ecclesiastical, get in the way of
personal help and love which, to be effective, have to be
infinitely varied and direct in their manifestations. In
societies where a rapidly increasing volume of material
wealth is made a kind of barometer by which to measure
the utility of individuals, groups and institutions, men,
even if they are clerics, are not unnaturally inclined to
judge religious institutions, and sometimes the religion
that is in their keeping, almost exclusively in these materialistic terms.

The tendency to regard economic growth as the test of
progress explains the preoccupation of some recent
scholars with religion and wealth. Such a preoccupation
turns upside down the true function of religion. It has
led to the adoption in the modern world of points of view

which can be admitted only with difficulty into the realm of spiritual experience.

These points of view may perhaps be divided into two categories. There is, first, the disposition to regard religions of every kind, partly because of their spiritual foundations, as the enemies of economic progress. It is to some extent as a consequence of this view that men turned away from organized religious worship during the nineteenth and early twentieth centuries. There is, secondly, the disposition to shape the policies of ecclesiastical foundations in order to aid material progress. Whatever the importance of material progress, and I am disposed to agree that this importance is great, it is a deformation of the Gospel to make such progress the ultimate goal of existence. In doing just that, the holders of this second point of view have encouraged the widespread assumption that material progress is the basis of all progress, including spiritual progress.

Neither of these points of view is likely to be of much help to the human welfare we seek in a greater understanding that will prevent total war. The Gospel suggests, and the recent experience of disinterested persons of discernment seems to support the suggestion, that materialism may become its own worst enemy. If that be true, material success cannot be a sound principle for determining the value of religious worship. ". . . Seek ye first the kingdom of God, and his righteousness," are the words of Our Lord, "and all these things shall be added unto you."*

The justification, in a worldly sense, for an ecclesiasti-

_____
* Matthew, VI, 33.

110

cal polity and state lies in making our inner lives rich in virtuous ways—in beauty, in truth and in love. This means a sharing of these riches with others, especially with those who are closest to us, and through these with others who are close to them. Would not this enrichment also provide the *religious* justification for an ecclesiastical polity and state?

According to Christian theology, what makes charity the first of the virtues, is that it is the only one which is the same here and in heaven. It is consequently of all the virtues the one that links man most closely to God. So the qualities essential to charity are independent of worldly wealth, and should be a guide to the way in which wealth is employed. If charity and love become guides, that is the surest way of making the eternal values count in the temporal world. Does not the recognition of the eternal, as the first goal of civilization, depend on a growing harmony in individuals with the divine will through love for others? In order to gain love it is necessary to deserve it. The way to deserve it is to give it, not for the sake of any return but for the sake of loving itself.

CHAPTER VI

Religion and the Founder

THE READER may want to be reminded that the word "civilization" in this essay always carries its eighteenth-century meaning. Its earliest use is said to be French. It is found in a book which the Marquis de Mirabeau published in 1757. For Mirabeau and his contemporaries, English as well as French, there were not, as for Gobineau, Spengler and Toynbee, several civilizations. There was one, and that was in process of being created among the Europeans in Europe and overseas. The fresh confidence in man, which was encouraging scientists to put their discoveries to practical use, was inspiring some political thinkers and historians to suppose that all Europeans, and eventually all nations and races, shared fundamental purposes of improvement capable of uniting them. Some of the greatest eighteenth-century writers—Montesquieu, Gibbon, Burke—felt that Europe was already what Burke called a "great republic." Their republic transcended every European frontier at a time when, in addition to national states, there were, especially in Germany and Italy, a host of small units each claiming sovereign rights.

The union of which Burke and others were conscious was not organized. It was not formulated in any rules. It was written on the hearts of men, because it was believed to rest, not on force, but on the intelligence and on the manners and conventions adopted by an elite who were capable of communicating with each other through a common language and the free acceptance of generally understood customs and beliefs, spiritual in origin.

The novel confidence in the capacity of human nature to improve, and the conventions and habits relating both to private life and international relations which went with this confidence, seem to have been largely lost in the late nineteenth and twentieth centuries, during the times of world wars, in spite of the astounding material success of the past hundred and fifty years. Apparently governments are no longer going to disown their spies. Informers are even to be accorded by the organs of publicity a fame which in their hearts persons of integrity reserve for courage which seeks no reward, no fame, and which is not discolored by any meanness in its methods. This is deeply disturbing. As we have just seen, it was a confidence that genuine virtue is self-justifying which gave our ancestors, in the eighteenth century and afterwards, an assurance that our race would use for good any powers that scientific and technological discovery might make available. It was on such assurances that industrialism was reared. This hope in man was held by many influential persons whose convictions counted, including some of the leading statesmen of the eighteenth century. Unlike the more recent students of society, they felt that knowledge gave access to something approaching universal principles upon which all could agree.

of industrialism were inseparable from Christianity, from the attempts made by our ancestors, Christian believers and nonbelievers alike, to give body to Christian ethics in both private and public relations, can we welcome the decline in the strength of the Christian faith that has characterized history since the eighteenth century? Is not this decline related to the loss of those generally understood customs and beliefs, those conventions concerning private conduct and international relations, which men of learning and culture had in common during the eighteenth century and afterwards?.

Was the attempt to live more than ever before in the spirit of the Gospel merely a useful device for getting industrial civilization launched or has it permanent value? If neither the discoveries of scientists nor the triumph of industrialism have shown that Christian belief is false, need the hopes which Christianity is capable of arousing be abandoned?

Possibilities for redemption are inexhaustible. The strength we sometimes find within ourselves to make an effort, to surmount obstacles, is ours by the grace of God. We can find something of the perfection which we lack with His help. These nonmaterial resources, present in the inner lives of individuals, have never been so needed as they are today. It is not modern science, but the insights we are offered by eternal truth, which might provide us with means partially to fill that vast gap in our knowledge which science has left by cutting out of its picture of the universe much that is "close to our heart."

Is there a road to faith other than the route of the cross and the route of love, two paths which so continuously interlace that they are inseparable? I do not exclude the possibility of finding other ways. All I suggest is that these ways are valid, and that all life, including university life, suffers when they are stifled. Combined, these ways can help persons to find the courage and the confidence which make it possible to surmount worldly obstacles in the conviction that they live in the service of something bigger and stronger than themselves. By keeping faith in these ways, what we have in us that is best and most honest is gained forever.

Is not the search for civilization, then, inseparable from the search for a more Christian world? Why do people find it so difficult to believe in this interrelationship? It is partly because they see Christianity through the weaknesses of priests, through the lack not only of charity and love but of justice in some of the rules and regulations that priests have made and that other priests enforce. It is partly because they see Christianity through the discourses and discussions of theologians and these lack for them the homely simple meaning for which they hunger. They forget that, for the believer, Christ is not a theologian, that He is not a man, that He is the Son of God. They rightly distrust human beings. But we are all men or women, and so our only hope is, at the same time, to trust them. If we are not often very inspiring creatures, it is surely disastrous to lose faith in our possibilities. The overwhelming question is not what man has been, or even what he is, but what he might become with the help of Christ. The question is whether, through the birth and growth of what Simone Weil calls a new idea of grandeur, the temporal world can be made

116

more Christian in spirit than it has ever been before.

An historian can perhaps assemble some material for those who would like to contribute to a more Christian world. He can make it clearer why Christianity has repeatedly gone shipwreck amid the treacherous icebergs that are always encountered in the evolution of men and of societies. In so doing, he can distinguish, as I am trying to in this essay, between the Light which Christ brought into the world, and the institutions founded by men and administered by other men. Christ is beyond shipwreck; and so Christianity is always ready to set out to sea again.

Through the Gospel Our Lord reveals, in absolute purity, some of the struggles of the perfect Soul confronted with the experiences of the temporal world. He teaches us that honesty and charity are right whether they lead to worldly recognition, to temporal success, or not. In a world where so many people are losing their balance and where words are losing any clear meaning, the qualities of honesty and charity may be called selfishness. This has always been so, and the lesson of history is that, in spite of it, those qualities ought to be cultivated more than ever in our industrialized world. Were not the charity and love of the Savior the cause of His persecution and crucifixion? Did not the Jews protest when Pontius Pilate referred to Christ as their king? Why should it be assumed that there is, in our present irreligious world, any close connection between the deeper virtues and public acclaim? When we falter in our duty out of fear of any kind, nothing can sustain us so much as an inner confidence, which transcends the

117

ego, that we are following, however humbly and inadequately, in Christ's footsteps. Nothing can sustain us so much as the confidence that we are striving to act here on earth according to the Light He has provided for us, and not out of any desire to advance ourselves according to the fragile and fleeting fashions of this world.

As Saint François de Sales says in his benign way, devotion is a sort of sugar that helps make palatable the difficult acts of life—those which we make in response to duty rather than to self-interest. Prayer and faith, which are part of devotion, remove some of the bitterness, some of the suffering, that accompany such acts; they even infuse into the pain elements of unpretentious satisfaction. "[Devotion] serves for fire in winter and for dew in summer; it knows how to abound and how to suffer poverty; it renders equally useful honour and contempt; it receives pleasure and pain with a heart almost always the same, and fills us with a marvelous content."* Nothing helps a person so much to assume the right responsibilities, to take a course that is difficult or unpopular but indispensable, as the belief that an all-wise Being is at his side. This can lead him to turn, in the midst of the hit-and-run life of our times, from the course that is easy or popular or that seems likely to save his skin, but that is dishonorable, unjust, unwise or cowardly.

Again and again the world has underestimated, and now more than ever under the glare of publicity and with

---

* *Introduction to the Devout Life*, trans. Allan Ross (London, 1937), p. 7. I have changed several words in the translation, in order better to fulfill the meaning, as I see it.

118

the derision furnished by debunkers, the value of wisdom and the beauty of love as personified in human beings; and where else than in them are we to find these values? People see in the searchers after wisdom and love faults and weaknesses which they are the first to acknowledge. Faults and weaknesses in honest persons are the inevitable consequence of imperfection. Yet how unimportant are these blemishes in comparison with the disaster that follows the abdication of an inner life that is repelled by the existence of sin, that tries honestly to distinguish evil from good, and that seeks to serve the neighbor.

Only such efforts as these to rise out of ourselves can provide an ultimate bulwark against totalitarianism. By identifying the barrier against the exercise of arbitrary power with the Supreme Being, who is wholly good, as Christianity has done, restraints on violence are given a firmer foundation and the subjects have better protection from a dictator and from all smaller forms of dictatorship. The ancient Greeks believed that jealous gods would punish civil tyrants and conquerors, when they usurped a power which does not properly belong to men. The Christian explanation of the fate that awaits these cruel men is far nobler. Their punishment comes not as vengeance—for God is not a man and cannot take offense, as a man does, at what men do—but as the consequences of sin. Punishment comes to them not because they have acted in place of God, but because they have acted in a way that is alien to His nature. Thus faith acts as a restraint on tyranny and conquest. John Donne explains the situation in a few lines.

That thou mayest rightly obey power, her bounds know;
Those past, her nature, and name is chang'd; to be
Then humble to her is idolatrie.
As streames are, Power is; those blest flowers that dwell
At the rough streames calme head, thrive and do well,
But having left their roots, and themselves given
To the streames tyrannous rage, alas are driven
Through mills, and rockes, and woods, and at last, almost
Consum'd in going, in the sea are lost:
So perish Soules, which more chuse mens unjust
Power from God claym'd, then God himselfe to trust.*

What is even worse for man's future than trusting "power from God claym'd" is something of which men in Donne's time had less experience than in ours. It is trusting power claimed from the mob.

It is doubtful whether in the whole of history the worldly case for a society animated by the spirit of Christ has ever been as strong as today. But the conditions which stand in the way of recognizing that the evolution of such a society could provide the basis for a movement towards human solidarity are manifold. The overwhelming majority of men are not Christian. Even those who are honest in professing to be, are almost invariably men first and Christians afterwards. I do not mean that they are not members of the Roman Catholic Church or of some other church founded in the name of Christ, whether it be Orthodox, Anglican or Protestant. I mean they are not Christian in their hearts; some of them are not Christian even in inclination though they go regularly to Mass and take the sacraments. Forms and ritual

* "Satyre III," ll. 100-110, *The Poems of John Donne,* ed. H. J. C. Grierson (Oxford, 1912), I, 158.

120

alone seem to matter to them; they do not seek the inspiration and the guidance in their lives that an independent adherence to truth, honor and love alone can provide.

So the non-Christian spirit which dominates the world is by no means the monopoly of those who profess other religions than Christianity or who remain independent of any religious affiliation. It is found only too often among those who practice the Christian faith.* That is why it seems necessary to begin by setting aside other reasons for the absence of Christ from the temporal world, in spite of their great importance, and to consider the weaknesses of religious institutions. These are not ordinary times. If, as seems evident, the organization of worldly institutions, including religious institutions, gets in the way of better human beings, everything needs to be done to break the red tape and the forms that prevent the best men have to offer from counting.

During the eighteenth and nineteenth centuries many of our ancestors looked with increasing horror upon the excesses of the clergy. They occasionally painted pictures of these iniquities which were far from just. Some of our contemporaries have embellished these pictures. Still, even when we allow for exaggerations, it remains true that plenty of acts of the clergy have been far from Christian. It remains true that the Gospel has frequently been interpreted by priests and pastors who not only lacked wisdom, but charity and love. The association of the Gospel with harshness and injustice is a great obstacle to the spread of the faith in a form that will

* Compare above, pp. 12-13.

121

strengthen those who have it in this testing time on earth.

Churches have often much to do with the education of the young. They are custodians of the most sublime aspirations of man. These conditions impose on clergymen a special responsibility and offer them a unique opportunity. There is an important sense in which it is more serious to have a man betray his mission when he represents God than when he represents Caesar. That is why the consequences of weakness and blindness in clergymen are especially disillusioning to those who are seeking a decent world society, which alone could meet the challenge of the scientific and technological successes of our times.

Not long ago a priest, who is a good man and who has had a respectable career, used these terrible words in a conversation that I witnessed: "The Church is not concerned with justice." Seeing that he had shocked his interlocutor, he added, "This isn't our fault. Canon law is derived from the Gospel. It is Our Lord who is responsible." In no way do I deny the need for canon law, or for papal authority, in matters of faith and morals. But it should be always remembered that canon law, and all ecclesiastical rules, ordonnances and decrees, have been the work of men; and that in this work these men have not always been inspired by Christ. There is nothing surprising in this. At the time of His crucifixion, not all His disciples had the courage to avow their faith. If, as individuals, we are seldom equal to the mission of representing Him, it is hardly possible to look for perfection in any institution founded and maintained by mortal men.

This is why the advice of the Savior to His disciples, as reported by Saint Luke, seems infinitely precious. "He that is not against us is for us." The importance of a collectivity that later became the Church is fundamental to the future of the Christian religion. But absolute faith, absolute fidelity, is due to God. "He that is not with me is against me; and he that gathereth not with me scattereth."*

At its best the Reformation represented an effort to mitigate the evils of the Roman Catholic Church as an institution organized and administered by sinful men, by establishing a more direct relationship between the individual and Christ. Believers were to be partly relieved from their dependence on priests for religious instruction and guidance. To the extent that the rise of Protestantism is consistent with the maintenance of faith in Our Lord, and an understanding of the truths He taught, there is much to recommend the individualism that it has nourished. Protestants were not altogether on the wrong track in seeking to reduce the emphasis laid by so many priests on conformity to ritual and man-made rules as the basis for salvation. The trouble has been that the diminution in the sacramental nature of worship, encouraged in varying degrees by the different Protestant sects, often diminished confidence in the Holy Presence. In so far as this happened, the closer relationship to Christ, that the Reformers sought, was not achieved.

* Luke, 9:50; 11:23.

The individual lost the very power of direct communion with God, in the name of which many Protestant sects were founded, because he was deprived of that cooperation in communion which the most saintly priests supply, and so of the more personal relationship to the faith which such priests facilitate. While personal integrity is the soul of love, and while personal integrity is nourished by a measure of independence and silence, loneliness can never be the food of love. Love always diminishes loneliness and pride. In kindling love we all need human help.

What, moreover, would have happened to the Christian message if no church had ever been founded to maintain and propagate the universal faith? In a world peopled by millions of men and women, as our world was even before the coming of civilization and industrialism and even before the coming of a European society, institutions of a kind which often lend themselves to unintelligent orthodoxy, and so to corruption and violence, were no doubt necessary to keep alive the knowledge of Christ and His teachings. The contribution of unity of worship to a faith whose *raison d'etre* is its universality is very great. The importance of a single Communion is brought out in some words written a hundred years ago by James Anthony Froude, who was not a Roman Catholic, and who was writing a history of England in which the Reformation provided a prominent theme. "Then, now, and ever," he says, "it was, and remains true, that in this great matter of religion, in which to be right is the first condition of being right in anything—not variety of opinion, but unity—not the equal

license of the wise and the foolish to choose their belief—
but an ordered harmony, where wisdom prescribes a
law to ignorance, is the rule which reasonable men
should most desire for themselves and for mankind."*

The question whether among the Western nations,
with their common Christian origins, the nonpracticing
citizens and even the nonbelieving citizens do not often
conduct themselves better, in moral and spiritual matters, than practicing Catholics, does not go to the heart
of the problem. The capital question is whether men and
women generally are not better than they would otherwise be because of a knowledge of the ethical principles
nourished by the Christian faith, which Christian
churches have done so much to preserve and to renew
for almost twenty centuries.

It is difficult to imagine that the new law, introduced
by Our Lord into the world, could have been kept alive
as it was in the Roman Empire, and extended during the
Dark Ages that followed, without church organization.
We can hardly be sure, as some of our agnostic ancestors
of the eighteenth and nineteenth centuries were, that
the price humanity has paid in cruelty and heartless dog-
matism for the Roman Church (and for other churches)
was too high. We have lived to see men tortured and
killed, without benefit even of the martyrdom that was
sometimes granted to heretics. We have to admit that
the avowed purpose of religious persecutions was less
ghastly than that of recent political persecutions. By
burning heretics, handed over as they often were for ex-

* J. A. Froude, *History of England from the Fall of Wolsey to the
Defeat of the Spanish Armada,* London, 1870, vol. iii, p. 62.

ecution to secular authorities, priests claimed they were saving a much larger number of human beings from worse sufferings after death. Furthermore physical cruelty was far less exceptional in all relations among the Western peoples in medieval times than it had become on the eve of the modern political persecutions, which is to say at the end of the nineteenth century. The improvement of manners was brought about by the inner light fostered in individuals through the love Christ introduced into the world. By helping to preserve that love, Christian churches helped to create the standards by which men came to condemn the iniquities of the Inquisition.

What then shall we say of the Reformation and the hopes it has aroused, and has sometimes partially fulfilled, of a more Christian ecclesiastical organization, of more Christian ecclesiastical authority? The Reformation, not least by its influence on certain Roman Catholics (among whom we have given as an example François de Sales), did much for Christianity, for the coming of civilization and the triumph of industrialism. Protestant missionaries were sometimes more straightforward and even more humane than Catholic missionaries. Yet pushed to its logical extreme, Protestantism leaves it open to every man to adopt his own interpretation of truth. In embracing this possibility, many a Protestant has a foil of unbelievers whose influence deprives him of the freedom to attach himself to Christ. The fact that he does not recognize his loss does nothing to restore the hope which has been taken from him.

It is hardly possible to conceive of the society that we

seek as the basis for a future world civilization without a church. Why a single church? If trust in the Christian ethics is the true hope for all human beings, it is not helpful to have the faith that is the basis of those ethics represented by an increasing number of independent churches, each in competition with the others. The kind of competition that now exists between churches contributes little or nothing to the creative diversity indispensable for human progress. The present-day scramble for communicants, notably in the United States where there are so many churches, too often resembles the rivalry between large department stores, each seeking a more numerous clientele for its prefabricated products. It even resembles the rushing of college students for fraternities. In the competition for communicants, Christianity is sometimes almost turned inside out and made into a means for maintaining a church, whereas the final purpose of any Christian church would seem to be to maintain Christ and provide consolation for suffering men. The rich diversity of interpretation that can strengthen the love the Lord evokes in us could be all represented within the framework of one church. Benjamin Franklin's words, ". . . vital religion has always suffered when orthodoxy is more regarded than virtue,"* contain much wisdom. And many competing orthodoxies are more likely to lead their sponsors to forget virtue than to recognize that all of these orthodoxies have their reason for existing in a single belief.

---

* As quoted by Conyers Read, "The English Elements in Benjamin Franklin," *Pennsylvania Magazine of History and Biography,* July, 1940, p. 321.

It is often said that no fixed belief is possible in the industrialized world, where, not only conditions, but also the knowledge men are gaining continually change; where, it is alleged, the only general truth is that all truth is relative.

This *is* a changing world and the conditions of justice, of love, of virtue *do* change with history. The world today *is* changing at an unprecedented speed. These circumstances add to the capital importance of a reconstruction of the laws and regulations of the church. (They add still more to the need that the clergy should be made up of better men.) By suggesting that the laws and regulations of the church need to be changed, I do not mean that the lessons and the spirit of Our Lord should be adjusted to changing worldly conditions and institutions. I mean rather that these conditions and these institutions need to be brought into a closer relation to the spirit of Christ, from which they have always strayed, and from which in some ways they stray today more than they have before. It is directly to Christ that the new conditions of the industrialized world need to be referred rather than to rules and regulations made by men under conditions which no longer exist. What truly wise person could claim that any church organization at present adequately provides the ordered harmony, with wisdom prescribing a law to ignorance, that Froude hoped to find in religious unity? No wise, no truly Christian priest could claim that his church has the monopoly of salvation. Nor could any truly Christian priest fail to believe that at least a minimum of Christian virtue, whether it is achieved within his church or without, is

128

more essential to salvation than ecclesiastical orthodoxy. The Day of Judgment is likely to be full of surprises!

The opportunities for the clergy are more far-reaching now than they have ever been. The adjustment, the reconstruction, which is so needed requires experience in the world, deep knowledge combined with creative imagination and love, and above everything a union with Christ that is almost superhuman. Great efforts which have been made in such a direction, whether by Protestants or Catholics, should now be renewed on a world scale with an awareness that the tangible problems today differ from those which have hitherto occupied the leading minds, including the leading ecclesiastical minds.

The peoples of the world are in need of Christ. They are in need of religious unity, in an age full of fads and fake religions. But, if we are not altogether mistaken, they need neither materialism nor a compromise with political persecution in the guise of religion. Whether or how the great need for firm belief can be filled is something no man can foresee. It can be filled only if those who have the Christian faith in their keeping (ecclesiastics and laymen alike) succeed in rising above the limitations of our time, and convince men everywhere, who are groping towards the good, that this faith is at once true, divine, eternal, that it is above all compassionate and loving. Emphasis should be laid more on substance than on form. Men should be welcomed into the faith less because of the opportunity of saving their souls and more as a means of saving the well-being of suffering and ill-guided humanity. Religious leaders will have to

129

be on the side of the humble and disinterested, whatever their riches and position may be. A church must come forward not primarily as a political but as a religious power, strong and courageous enough to serve the spiritual freedom for which Christianity at its best has always stood. It will have to reconsider, not only the world, but church organization and power itself, in relation to the words: "But many that are first shall be last; and the last first."*

The primary end of civilization is not the dignity of man. It is the dignity of God in man. And the great renewal to which we are summoned is not only an affair for the churches. Men must retain their independence, because what is needed above all is a wise human renewal. The objective is as simple as the climb towards it is steep and almost hopelessly difficult. How can men and women, each according to their nature, become better than they are? How can they become more worthy of their Creator than they have ever been before? Faith can gain strength only as a manifestation of the beauty and virtue of which human beings have sometimes shown themselves to be capable. It is beauty and virtue, which should guide men towards efforts to make the world more Christian, that concern us in the rest of this essay. Religious practices need to be made over in the light of purer visions of the beautiful and the good.

* Matthew, XIX:30; Mark, X, 31.

PART III: BEAUTY

CHAPTER VII

Art and Life

POLITICAL ECONOMY or economics, as we know it, is a relatively new subject. Its origin can hardly be traced back beyond the late sixteenth century. That was the time of those great changes in methods of intellectual inquiry which set science on its astounding modern course of development. It was also the time when technological problems associated with the exploitation of coal mines for the first time demanded solutions leading eventually to steam power, railways, cheap iron and steel. The birth of economics is linked in time, therefore, with that of the industrialism, created in Europe and America, which dominates the world today.

It is almost an axiom of theoretical economics that general overproduction is inconceivable. While it is admitted that an individual or a society may produce more of certain products than are wanted, desires it is said have no limit. Consequently the aim of economic endeavor should be to increase, as far as possible, the production of goods and services; the purpose of economic theory should be to discover and reveal new roads to economic growth.

There have been nevertheless some economists who believed that their inquiry should extend to desires other than the material and the quantitative. Such a one was the late Philip Wicksteed who began his career as a medievalist and participated in a much read prose translation of Dante. For Wicksteed it was legitimate and necessary that the economist take into account all human needs: the spiritual, artistic and ethical as well as the material. And indeed can these needs be separated? Can the body be happy if the soul is sad? Can it be assumed, as political leaders and civil servants (along with businessmen and economists) seem in their policies almost to take for granted, that if greater quantities of commodities are produced and if life is lengthened, the condition of the individual will automatically improve?

The comfort and peace of a well-balanced household does not depend only on the quantity of products installed and consumed; it does not depend only on the size of the income. It depends, above all, on the quality of the satisfactions and the harmony of the family relations. Happiness cannot be measured, any more than love or courage can be bought.

To the historian it appears that the importance of the many and varied needs and desires of men and women has changed greatly with changes in time and place and status. The kinds of goods that are in demand are never quite the same under different conditions. It is possible to conceive of a community in which the supply of commodities and services produced by machinery and automation has become so large that they lose their attraction for an ever increasing proportion of the population to such an extent that purchases are reduced. It is also possible to conceive of a community in which the standardization of products, while increasing the output and contributing to economic growth, diminishes the happiness of a majority of the members.

During recent decades the rapidity with which capital has flowed into large-scale enterprises for the massive extraction of raw materials, for mass manufacture, transportation and communication and for mass sales bears some resemblance in its one-sidedness to the flow of capital in the Mediterranean world into large estates known as villas. The primary purpose of the ancient villa economy was the production of wine and olive oil. In the first century of the Roman Empire, province after province followed central Italy in converting arable and forest lands to vineyards and olive orchards. The driving force behind this economy was the thirst of landlords, the great majority of whom lived in cities, for profits from the sale of these products. The need of the classical peoples for olive oil and probably also for wine was greater than that of the Anglo-Saxon peoples of recent times. But there was a limit. Their appetites refused to be whetted beyond a certain point. Eventually both liquids became drugs on the market. The price they could command fell; sometimes buyers could hardly be found for them at any price. It was apparently for this reason that the system of investment and exchange and industrial management built on the villa economy collapsed. The investors had unwittingly pushed production in a single direction farther than human nature would bear. If, under such conditions, there are no alternative directions, the entire economy is undermined. Something very like that seems to have happened in the Roman Empire during and after the second and third centuries.

The material wants to which the modern economy of machinery and automation caters are no doubt much more extensive and in many ways healthier than those of the ancient villa economy. But the modern economy has taken on a special character of its own which may also have limits in so far as the satisfaction of the human person is concerned. Sensitive men and women are frequently distressed by the mechanical and quantitative tests, which have come to determine the decisions of businessmen, politicians, advertisers, purveyors of news and educators, with respect to the ways in which capital shall be used. In so far as private business is concerned the consumer can retain some independence; he is not forced to buy what he doesn't like. Yet there are plenty of influences in the modern economy which tell him what he should like. This is hammered into him by advertisers in the newspapers, over the radio and the television sets. But there is little to help him to discover for himself what he really likes. It is not always possible for him to refuse what he is offered. There may be no alternative product to buy. And in the case of those funds which are allocated mainly by government officials and the directors of private philanthropic agencies who manage other people's money, or by the administrators and faculties of universities, the consumers and the students are left with even less choice. They think they have no alternative to the kind of commodities, the kind of education and the kind of enjoyments that are ordered for them by foundations, legislators and functionaries.

So the range of selection essential to the cultivation of individual taste has been narrowed, until free choice is restricted mainly to persons with large incomes, of whom happily there are still a few.

The orientation of energy, time and thought in directions which cater to the least essential and most empty sides of our nature is probably causing much deeper and more widespread dissatisfaction than is realized. In the industrialized economy of our times men and women miss much that they really want. Really wanting takes time and experience and they seldom find either. They lack resources that could help them to rise out of themselves, to commune in ways that are helpful and delightful with their neighbors and their relatives. They find in what they are offered little to console them in their suffering or to sustain them in their faith, almost nothing on which to sharpen their wit. The economic systems welcomed by modern economics have helped in the wealthiest countries to reduce greatly the number of persons living in material misery. But they have done almost nothing to help the individual who wants to live a fuller life. At the same time these economic systems are encouraging the multiplication of population in those parts

135

of the world where it is least supportable. The economics of our times, which are accepted almost without question by those who teach economics (a "Marxist" economy in the communist countries and a supposedly "anti-Marxist" economy in the more democratic countries), are leading mainly towards societies of men and women starved in their inner lives. Even the most fortunate and successful among them find life exhilarating mainly in so far as they can keep busy and can close their eyes to the deeper ends of existence. The head of a great industrial enterprise, whose function it is to reduce costs in the interests of success, and who mechanizes and automatizes to the utmost in order to provide the stockholders with profits, is appalled to find that he is encouraging the kind of routine labor and consumption which, as a man of taste, he can sometimes hardly bear to contemplate.

The expansion of markets in the industrialized economy which is now spreading from North America and Western Europe to the rest of the planet—to Russia already, and tomorrow, it would seem, to China—has been based less and less on either urgent needs or refined tastes, more and more on largely manufactured desires. The proportion of the population in the countries where civilization and industrialism originated, who take an active part in creative work or in creative entertainment, has also decreased rapidly in the last fifty years. The result has been a great increase in synthetically generated activity undertaken in the hope of escaping boredom. Mechanical responses and inner emptiness are the price we are paying for the multiplication of commodi-

ties and people, at a time when societies have an unprecedented need for an excess of the rare individual
qualities of authentic choice and leadership.

It is at a considerable price, therefore, that men have
discovered in recent decades by the use of medicines
and sanitation, by changes in fashion, in the materials
used for construction, and by advertising, means of multiplying consumers and consumption as never before in
history. The uneasiness which the new conditions generate is perhaps deeper and more widespread in the
United States than in Europe.

In the country which is generally supposed—not altogether without justification—to be mainly responsible
for the drab, tasteless nature of modern life, the dissatisfaction over the results of quantitative progress, of economic growth measured in volume, is perhaps becoming
more serious than anywhere else.

From at least the mid-nineteenth century until after
the World War of 1914-18 the dream most characteristic
of American hopes was the dream of the infinitely large.
It was expressed in literature in a masterpiece of American imaginative prose, Melville's *Moby Dick*, published
in 1851. So far as I am aware, no earlier writer had made
a whale the hero of a novel. This was, I think, the first
time when a great work of art was constructed around
such a living colossus. What seems to be the explanation?

The image which long welled up in sensitive Americans was precisely that of the very big—railroads span-
ning a continent, enormous ships, airplanes climbing to
the moon. Among all living creatures the whale provides
best an image of the infinitely large. Like the idea of the

skyscraper, born at much the same time, *Moby Dick* is an example of peculiarly American genius.

At the end of the eighteenth century, soon after the founding of the United States, the Western world began to possess, as a result of industrial revolution, technical means capable of giving body to this dream. Nowhere else, it then seemed, was natural wealth so abundant as in North America. To a degree that was not true either in Europe or Asia, here was a virgin continent. Men who had the rapidly developing new technology at their disposal could start from scratch without any serious problem of tearing down in order to build. They had only to destroy buffaloes, antelopes, wolves, bears and, more reluctantly, some Indians; they had only to clean up swamps and combat the violent elements to get at vast new resources of the soil and subsoil, in order to find their El Dorado. Throughout the nineteenth century the efforts on this continent to exploit fresh sources of energy and to conquer nature with more effective power-driven machinery filled the imagination of American pioneers. The caravans broke their way through the wilderness—ever farther westward—as frontier was pushed beyond frontier. The frontier spirit, conceived in the image of the infinitely large, was expressed in the railways Americans laid, the companies they organized, the banks they floated. The race to conquer and unify a continent culminated in the results achieved by the first Henry Ford. He filled cities, towns and villages with cheap motorcars which enabled almost anyone to get almost anywhere over rough roads in a vast country deprived since the eighteen-eighties of the horizon of frontiers.

As city replaced country living, there disappeared something of the freedom and the adventure that had created the industrial United States, with its seas of factories and blast furnaces lighting the skies at night. From the point of view of material comfort city life was a great improvement on country life. Yet, in the new realizations, men and women lost the realities, the healthy earthiness, which country life and the movement westward in stagecoaches had often provided. Now that almost everything was big and getting bigger, the figure of the infinitely large lost some of its savor. Colossi began to circumscribe the individual spirit. What shrank increasingly, with the spread of the very big during the past fifty years, was the opportunity that the nineteenth-century quest had offered in its pioneering and country living for sympathy and friendship based on neighborliness, in spite (to some extent because) of the hardships and the bitter and sometimes violent competition combined with crime. Nor was it clear, as it had been to the adventurous captains of the nineteenth century, in what directions new authentic adventures could be found to quicken and satisfy imaginative men. The wild west wind continued to blow across the plains from a country beyond them which once had seemed almost pure magic. But the adventurers who had won the West, created the railroads, the mines, the banks and the newspapers, passed away. Their successors, who were often able and industrious, were obliged to deal on a gigantic scale with punier realities, leading, for all the difficulties of meeting them, to less human goals. By comparison, the new spirit of enterprise was chained and bowed. The Boeing 707's passed above the wind or ploughed through it, but men and women were less a part of it, just as their new view of alps from above deprived them of some of the grandeur that confronts the mountaineer painstakingly cutting steps in steep glaciers or squeezing his way inch by inch up rocky chimneys.

·It is not surprising, therefore, that new dreams, embodying the hopes of the most sensitive Americans, are different, especially since the depression of 1929-33 and the War of 1939-45. The most adventurous spirits are disillusioned by the infinitely large, by mechanized leisure and mass consumption. They have begun to have industrialism on their conscience, to search for alternatives to science and technology. Since 1942, when I published a book called *The United States and Civilization*, dissatisfaction over the results of mechanization and automation has been reflected in an increasing number of publications and in various ventures undertaken to "humanize" the population both by elementary and by adult education.

In this disillusionment there is perhaps hope of constructive building. The reservations that sensitive persons are beginning to have concerning the value of an economy which produces almost exclusively for the purpose of producing more and of keeping people busy, regardless of its consequences for the individual's delight, might lead to a skepticism of skepticism itself, now that skepticism has lost its constructive side to become a cloak for cynicism. These reservations might lead to efforts to build a world society to transcend the partial societies that hitherto have embodied all men's energies.

The efforts that are being made to encourage taste

lead us to ask what art can do for man, what it can do to help in the search for civilization. Industrialism has come to stay, unless human beings destroy it with the new weapons which have accompanied its triumph. This means we must welcome its spread to those regions of the globe that have not yet got it, as a means of helping to raise all peoples who want to be raised out of material misery. The problem of making better men is all the more urgent on that account. And the leadership in this matter is up to the Western peoples, who bear the main responsibility for the kind of world in which we live.

Can the service of the beautiful help to nourish such leadership? If we are to consider that question, we have to ask what relation has art to life? To science? To faith? And, finally, what relation has it to virtue?

The experiences that are the most important to human beings as individuals—and as an historian I would go farther and say to the evolution and the future of our race—are experiences that in the fullest sense cannot be communicated through art. They can only be lived. And they can be lived fully, and that in very rare cases and in a way only for moments, by two persons, a woman and a man together.

They cannot be repeated, though the glow they produce is indestructible and is capable of being at least partially transmitted to many others, who share in the pleasure and warmth which great happiness and great beauty alone can diffuse. Though new and equally meaningful experiences can come—must come as the relationship grows—particular moments of this kind are unique. Great artists have sometimes managed to preserve something of them as parts of their works. Once fixed in a work of living art, they are there for others to contemplate, and they are capable of making so real an impression on a person who reads or sees the work that it sometimes becomes difficult for him to distinguish them from similar moments in his own life. It is as if he had lived them himself. But living them through the artist's version is never the same experience as living them directly.

Such moments in life spring up within us, sometimes without preparation, though almost always out of materials and earlier experiences some of which may be aroused by works of art. Years ago a young friend of mine who had been brought up an atheist, in listening to a performance in Paris of Bach's Saint Matthew Passion, acquired a belief in the possible truth of the Christian Gospel. The words and music conveyed to him with overwhelming force that it was evil, of which he was beginning to feel the hurt, that had brought the suffering and crucifixion of Christ. He recognized that any sensitive person, who is trying to lead a pure life, might be wounded in a similar way. He felt that it is the divine side of man that causes him to suffer. He felt that it is the divinity of Christ and the absence of all sin that made Him suffer more than anyone else. He saw that it was Christ's triumph over this suffering that reveals Him as unique, universal and eternal. "He that loseth his life for my sake shall find it," are words of the Gospel.° The meaning of finding in giving, of loving in suffering, was brought home to my young friend for the first time by the musical dramatization of the passion, death and

° Matthew X:39.

resurrection, as Bach presented them that night through his interpreters.

I am not suggesting that all the listeners to Bach's music on that occasion had a similar experience. My friend told me of personal events that he thought might have contributed to his response to the music. First were his childhood relations with his grandmother. Alone among the persons who brought him up, she believed in the divinity of Christ and impressed him with this belief. Secondly, he told me that one night, as a child, he remembered Christ had appeared to him in a kind of dream. Finally, the meaning of the Saint Matthew Passion dawned upon him because he was in most intimate communion with a woman whose sufferings in the presence of evil were intense to the point of exaggeration. She was with him at the concert, and the moment came as part of his experience with her.

Moments like those which he lived that evening cannot be premeditated or arranged. Although the elements are present in the subconscious, the manner in which they combine is beyond logical explanation. That is why such moments cannot be photographed, reproduced, recorded or televised, as works of art can be. If a doctor tried, as an experiment, to produce one, an essential ingredient would be absent. It is surprise. The shock of surprise is integral in the experience. That shock takes the place of positive evidence and brings the certainty a person feels in the truth of what the instant has revealed, and what no later instant can reverse. Inner certainty takes the place of experiment and observation which bring the scientist objective certainty.

143

Such moments are capable of changing the direction of a life. They are capable of creating new persons. How do they influence others who do not participate? Partly through the example set by the new persons. Partly through the leadership they exercise in small ways and in large, according to the positions they occupy. Partly through the beauty that those who are artists create, helped by having themselves lived such experiences. In any case the significance of these moments cannot be taught in the ways that positive scientific knowledge is effectively taught. Truth is in the images that form in the minds of others through the example set by the innovators, and such images are never identical with the experiences which gave birth to the example.

These deepest moments in life partly resemble and partly differ from works of art. They differ because they are less planned, and because they result most often from a unique interrelationship between two persons, whereas a work of art can be achieved only through more conscious preparation by a single person, a preparation that involves training in an appropriate artistic technique. But they also resemble great works of art. Such a work carries the artist along with it. In the process of creating it, he is moved by flashes of intuitive insight and by inner judgments which are sometimes as little premeditated, and as difficult to explain in positive language, or to demonstrate scientifically, as are the greatest moments between two lovers. If an artist tries to reproduce or to define moments of lived perfection by means of brush strokes or notes or even by words, he fails as an artist. Yet, though this appears to be contradictory, such moments are the stuff of the most moving art. Unless the artist has lived them and is able to transfuse their essence into the stories he tells, the poems he writes, the symphonies he composes, he can hardly achieve the heights of beauty and truth. I think it was Goethe who said that the unique is the universal. It is a Goethe, a Shakespeare or a Dante who is able, as the result of a kind of inner dialogue, to snatch out of eternity something of the richness, the freshness and the permanence vouchsafed to him and to some other human beings in the unique moments of life.

The weakness of much that passes for art in our times is to be found in the fact that the artist has lost touch with life. It is also to be found in the fact that he has lost touch with the good, with virtue. The difficulties in bringing life and art together are immense, those of bringing virtue and art together are even more so. Yet both unions are essential for the future of man's freedom and man's dignity under God.

All art, particularly perhaps the art of poetry, is formal; works of art must be made out of words and sounds, lines and colors, bronze and stone. Training in technique is vital. Mr. T. S. Eliot was recently subjected to an interesting press conference when he and his wife were guests in my apartment. A newspaper correspondent asked him what he thought of Picasso. One of the most moving of Picasso's drawings of a woman seated—a kind of female Moses—was hanging on the wall behind Eliot, as if to give force to his reply. This is what he said, "Picasso is a very great artist. But, before taking his liberties, he was a superb, a supreme draftsman."

The picture also showed that technique is not enough for greatness. Why is this? It is because words, notes, lines or brush strokes, once down and released by their authors, are fixed and unchangeable. Yet this does not kill the life which the greatest artists manage to create by making the technique they have learned their servant, by mastering technique and not letting it master the gifts they derive from God, not letting it damp the divine fire His gift has helped them to light within themselves.

What do we mean when we say that an artist creates life, that a work of his is living? We mean partly at least that it can be lived by and through those who experience it, as well as by the artist who lives in creating it and who ceases to live by it in that sense when it is finished (however much money it brings him and it seldom brings much). Once his work is launched, its connection with its creator is lost, save in so far as he directs or guides the performers or interpreters, or is able to revise what he has done. After the artist has ceased to concern himself with a particular work, the only direct connections which it has are with its public, and with those who interpret it for a public.

In a sense, therefore, a work of art is fixed. But in another sense the most marvelous works of art are continually in movement, by the exaltation they kindle and the discoveries they facilitate. How is it that the great artist manages to escape from the prison to which all craftsmen are condemned because of the formal rules of their craft and because of the necessity they are under to finish one composition and start another? It is by a force, divine in origin, which is the source of the most wonderful human acts. Faith in that source might bring about a new hope in the capacity of the human person to attain some of the perfection that science is incapable of helping him achieve, though scientific results have a perfection of a different kind. During about four centuries, the grand strategy of the natural sciences and of mathematics has been to simplify problems with a view to achieving certainty in ever more rigorously restricted realms. By so doing, as Schrödinger writes, science has adopted a means of extending knowledge at the expense of cutting "our own personality out, removing it."

It is not simple, clear-cut problems, but most complicated problems of our personality, that are in vital need of solution to prevent the atomic age from becoming a nightmare.* And because of their complicated nature these personal problems cannot be solved once and for all. There is no such exact answer as there is to specific scientific and mathematical problems. Nor can the tentative answers be applied directly, as solutions can be in science, to technological methods of dealing with affairs in the practical realm. That is because the answers are of a different order, and their applications are not mechanical and material, but personal. The only answer is not a generally valid answer; it is the answer an individual, faced with choices in life, has to make. The question is whether experiences acquired with the help of works of art can help us to make better choices. That is what they should do, because the complicated problems, which escape science, are the stuff of art.

An eminent physicist, the late Albert Michaelson, had

* See above, p. 41.

147

in him, like all great scientists, something of the artistic temperament (without which scientific originality would dry up). Once at a convention of scientists, he is said to have become exasperated by the pleas of his colleagues to organize group inquiries in scientific research. Rising, he told the astonished assembly, "Gentlemen I have a more constructive suggestion to make. I suggest we appoint a committee of one hundred to write the great American poem."

The absurdity of such a proposal will strike many, because the validity of the individual response is still recognized in art. Notwithstanding the efforts of dadaists, beatniks and other sects, which seem to be legion and whose influence is mainly destructive, the exclusion of the personality and of firm values, that has become so general in connection with university teaching and research, is incomplete in connection with art. In spite of efforts by governments to systematize and control it, the artistic life has not yet been organized entirely after the manner of academic departments and faculties.

The artist's purpose in simplifying is different from the natural scientist's; in some ways it is the antithesis of his. In his lines and colors, his notes or his words, the artist aims to achieve as great an economy, as great an inevitability, as possible. But this can never be effectively done by rendering the problems that he relates to his subject less complex than they are. These problems are not repeatable, though many similar problems flood human experience. In the uniqueness of each is their universality, so the essentials the artist seeks are those which help to reveal the complexities of the universal. If he

148

succeeds in finding those essentials, he may sometimes provide a guiding light for men and women of all classes, all races, all generations. Motives, passions, faith and hope are not ruled out of the artist's subject matter in so far as possible. Nor are they artificially simplified in an effort to convey a single precise message, whose meaning is unmistakable. That is because they are part of life, and life is changing and rich, and because art that is lifeless, whatever it may be, is never beautiful.

In 1950 Mr. T. S. Eliot conducted a seminar for the Committee on Social Thought, which I directed since it was established twenty years ago at the University of Chicago. The subject was his *Four Quartets*. Each of the poems was discussed by a different student. They put much zest into their work and brought forward their interpretations in the presence of the master, of other students and of members of the faculty, some of whom made observations on their own account. As a result we were confronted with several different interpretations of the same line in one of the poems. The audience appealed to Mr. Eliot. What did *he* mean by his words?

By an odd coincidence one of the persons who was present on that occasion a decade ago, wrote to me recently about this episode. Her recollection coincides with mine. This was Mr. Eliot's reply: "I really have forgotten just what I meant when I wrote that line." Then he added: "You are all right. I think I meant all those things." He went on to explain that the strength of poetry is in its richness, its diversity of meaning. And the good life is like that, full of inexhaustibly varied meaning. This richness in no way impairs, but rather augments,

149

the simple grandeur of the artistic impact upon the mind, the eye, the ear.

The contrast between the nature of the artistic and of the scientific result presents itself perhaps at least as forcibly in music as in poetry. It may almost be said that the more marvelous a musical composition, the more it is likely to strike the listener differently each time he hears it. That is what makes it possible for the greatest works of music to absorb their interpreter altogether, and, in doing so, to raise him from a simple performer to a musician touched by genius. The late Artur Schnabel was not only a pianist but a composer. As a pianist he played with a natural perfection which, for me at least, made his interpretations of the greatest works of piano music the most moving of recent times. In his maturity he performed 'only the compositions of Bach, Mozart, Beethoven, Schubert, Schumann and Brahms. He once explained to me why. As a youth, he had memorized the piano pieces of many other composers, among them those of Chopin. But he discovered that after he knew one of these pieces completely, he could play it, once and for all, as well as he felt it could be played. It was otherwise with the compositions he chose to perform. In interpreting again and again, almost endlessly, those of Mozart, Beethoven and Schubert he never succeeded in playing any as well as he wanted to play them, as well as he felt they could be played. By confining himself to these compositions, he acquired greater freedom and greater variety than a more extensive repertoire could have provided. It is concentration in depth that can give the endless richness the great artist is seeking. Everyone of Schnabel's concerts became a fresh experience for him and so for the sensitive listeners in his audience. Each time that he played, he could fall in love with his task. Falling in love with what is worth loving, whether it be in art or in life, is a necessary condition for creating beauty and conveying it to others.

In art the most satisfying simplification is one that leaves a rugged exterior. This is an exterior of which it is impossible to tire. It rewards constant re-examination because the result that has been obtained by the artist is mysterious and inexhaustible. It is the complexities embodied in what is made to appear simple (for the unwary or the insensitive to verge almost on the banal) that make a work of art permanently inspiring. While a consciousness of its beauty is likely to well up in a sensitive person at the first breathless meeting he has with it, the recognition of its many-sided significance grows on inspection and with repetition. It is somewhat as with love: the test of the authenticity of a work of art, as of a living object of devotion, is hidden in its capacity to withstand familiarity.

The roles of art and of science, then, in the future of man should be distinct. Both are indispensable. To some extent knowledge of science can enrich the artistic experience of the creative artist, as in the cases of Pascal and Goethe, just as, in a different way, works of art can fortify and inspire the scientist in his researches, as in the cases of Eddington and Einstein. The existing gap between what Sir Charles Snow calls the two cultures—art and science—is almost as scandalous as he suggests, and it ought to be bridged. But confusing the two

151

worlds, thinking that science can replace art, will not help to bridge it. Here, as in all the finest things men and women do, it is necessary to distinguish in order to unite.

An article illustrating the confusion which is helpful neither to science nor to art, appeared some years ago in an American newspaper. A journalist suggested that progress in advertising was becoming so rapid that the time was approaching when it would be "raised from an art to a science." Without touching the question whether so interested a calling as advertising can be either artistic or scientific in the deeper meaning of those words (where the self is enlisted not for the sake of private advantage but of beauty and truth) our discussions of religion and science and of religion and man lead us to distrust efforts to render art scientific. Such efforts do not serve either truth or beauty. They threaten to dehumanize our race.

This journalist's suggestion also indicates a misunderstanding of the hierarchy of human achievements, widespread today. The greatest scientists understand the limitations of their genius better. This is illustrated by an account I was recently given of Heisenberg's sojourn at Cambridge University. The discoverer of the scientific principle of indeterminacy is a gifted amateur musician. One night after dinner in hall he sat down at the piano. For the fellows of the college, lounging in their chairs, he played the last sonata of Beethoven, opus 111. From his playing something of the wonder of this work emerged which could not escape his listeners. Heisenberg finished the last movement amid silence created by the awe which great beauty alone can inspire. "There, gentlemen," he said quietly as the notes died away, "there you have the difference between science and art. If I had never lived someone else would have discovered the principle of indeterminacy. As modern science has evolved that discovery was inevitable. But if Beethoven had never lived, no one would have written this music."

Great art is related to those sides of our nature which, Schrödinger tells us, science cuts out of its pictures. It is concerned with good and bad, as well as beautiful and ugly, with love and hate, with eternity, with all that *is* close to our heart. Now, partly because of the sterilizing process to which the "misplaced concreteness" of the higher learning contributes, men and women are losing touch with the deeper sides of their nature.

Is it not necessary, therefore, for the sake of beauty as well as for the sake of faith, that men and women draw nearer to life, in order to make their experience more real, more concrete, to bring beauty into closer contact with material reality by fusing it with spiritual existence? For the salvation of the individual (and our race is meaningful through its individuals), art, like faith, and like ethics, has an importance that science lacks, and for which the scientific outlook and scientific methods of approaching experience are no substitute.

I hope I shall not be misunderstood. Therefore I should repeat that an artist can never provide direct solutions for practical problems. As an artist he cannot preach sermons or engage in propaganda for any social or political or economic or even scientific cause. Of what use is he then? It is now a very widely held opinion, encouraged by the spending of vast sums of money and

energy, that the activities of practical men and prop-
agandists alone are useful—that such men alone can
help us in divers ways to diminish the world's great evils:
misery, mental sickness, the danger of total war. But
these evils come from our nature. Analyzing them by
scientific methods provides information that can be of
much value in dealing with them. But science is neutral
so far as evil is concerned. It is only by improving our
nature, by taking account of our potentialities to serve
the good as such, and allowing persons to cultivate the
accuracy and precision that can come only from the
direct communication, to those close to them, of the
inner truths they have discovered through grace and
concentration, that a sense of balance, of measure, of
moderation, can be brought into the practical domain.

The late Professor Morris Cohen was fond of telling a
story of his days at Harvard when he was studying for
the doctor's degree in philosophy. A fellow graduate
student, a serious-minded young man, came to him one
evening, during their second year of residence in Cambridge, for a heart-to-heart talk. He told Cohen he was
greatly troubled, almost to the point of giving up graduate study, by a growing feeling that what he was learning was of no use. He had struggled to find a practical
purpose in it, but in vain. He felt he was missing something important. Cohen reassured him by saying simply
"it hasn't any use!"

The very great spiritual achievements have always
grown out of the conviction that they have to be done
whether or not they are useful. Dedication is aroused by
the faith that one has been vouchsafed an inner truth to

154

such a point that one wants above all else to seek a single goal, by most varied means, regardless of the consequences. In those moments of courage when men or women willingly risk their lives, when, by choice, they give all they have, they are guided by an overwhelming belief in the utility of the useless. Universality is based on that mysterious conviction, the validity of which transcends any possible positive demonstration. In the presence of truth, of beauty, of faith, in the presence of death and of love, we have only the useless—what we have done because we felt we must—to sustain us.

When the utility of the useless is recognized, it becomes plain that the creative artist is concerned with problems that are more vital for the future of humanity than scientific problems, or problems faced by specialists in what are called the social sciences, or problems met by businessmen. All these scholars and administrators and executives are tied down by the specific character of their assignments. They cannot wholeheartedly devote themselves as persons to becoming better men and women. The significance of the artist's effort, like that of the saint, for all its apparent uselessness, embraces the whole of human nature as exemplified in a single person. How then can the artist find the spiritual nourishment that he needs, that will enable him to face his task as an independent individual, dedicated only to beauty and truth?

Waste is one of the most striking and terrifying characteristics of industrialism. Nowhere perhaps is it so widespread as in the United States. The men who have vast sums at their disposal—political administrators, directors of so-called charitable foundations, presidents of

universities, heads of museums—take their advice mainly from scientists, from specialists in the social and
behavioral sciences, and from practical businessmen.
The advice they mainly rely on bolsters their own inclinations to spend other people's money on projects that
do nothing to fortify the individual in an effort to outdo
himself. They are inclined to hire scholars to work for
them rather than to encourage gifted persons to become
themselves. They go on the assumption that knowledge
is a substitute for character, instead of merely a tool
which can be used for evil as readily as for good.

It is necessary therefore to alter the outlook of those
who spend money on a vast scale. It is perhaps also desirable to diminish public expenditures in order to increase the private revenue of individuals. Nevertheless
nothing will be gained merely by transferring to individuals the spending power of government agencies and of
charitable foundations (which are often given money in
order to prevent its going to the government in taxes)
unless private citizens acquire a new outlook and a new
love for the good life. In so far as the artist encourages
such a change in the minds and purposes of individuals
by the works of beauty that he creates, he serves civilization. That is because works of art, capable of touching the
heart, can become powerful intruments for guiding
peoples and nations towards common understanding. In
music, in painting, in every visual art, a great work speaks
in a universal tongue which all can comprehend. It
surmounts the language barrier which makes it so difficult for works of literature to count except among those
whose language is the author's.

But the influence of works of art is not necessarily good. They can change human nature for the worse as well as for the better. Therefore it will be futile for the welfare of the race, to devote to the search for beauty a portion of the vast sums now spent on scientific and technological and administrative research, unless beauty and virtue can be brought closer together than ever before. Has the artist the power to become wiser and, by his example, to help more persons to become wise, to guide them towards juster, more charitable lives? Can art reinforce and give richer meaning to Christian ethics by helping to form men and women who fulfill themselves in ways that help the race?

Beauty is regarded in the industrial societies of our time as a luxury. It is supposed to be exclusive and expensive. Works of art are not infrequently compared by the vulgar, who are often also rich, to caviar. So it will be asked whether industrialized societies can afford to devote their energies to beauty, whether it is in the interest of the "masses" to do so; whether it is in the interest of national defense. Before considering the possible relation of delight to human improvement, then, it is necessary to consider its relation to wealth.

157

CHAPTER VIII

Art and Wealth

To WHAT EXTENT are there connections between the economic prosperity of human societies and the creation of beauty?

Historians have been struck sometimes by the apparent association of exceptionally rich artistic achievements with periods of remarkable material advance. One of the most striking examples is the flowering of Greek culture during the short sixty years between the Battle of Marathon in 490 B.C. and the outbreak of the Peloponnesian War in 431 B.C. During those six decades there worked at Athens, then only a small town according to the standards of population that prevail in our industrialized world, at least seven of the very greatest figures in the entire history of art and thought. If any competent judge since the Renaissance were asked to name the hundred leading artists and thinkers of all time, he could hardly omit Aeschylus, Phidias, Sophocles, Herodotus, Euripides, Thucydides or Socrates. All of them, except Aeschylus, were born between 500 and 470 B.C. All of them, except Aeschylus, who died probably in 456, were seen by most Athenians during the two decades 450-431.

In those twenty years the Parthenon, the Erechtheum and the Propylaea, with their marvelous embellishments, all went up on the Acropolis under the direction of Pericles (*ca.* 495-429), to form one of the most perfect groups of buildings ever conceived by man. There they stand, after twenty-four centuries of time, an example of the permanence of beauty.

The years between the Persian and the Peloponnesian Wars were an age of prosperity for the Greek city-states, and above all for Attica. The population was growing, new colonies were being founded overseas, the imports of grain and timber were mounting. The increases in wealth were stimulated by the supplies of silver that were being won from the recently discovered mines of argentiferous lead ore on the mountain of Laurion. There some of the shafts went down three hundred feet, an uncommon depth in those days at which to rake a livelihood, an uncommon depth anywhere before the Renaissance. The slopes and valleys were full of men washing, breaking and preparing the ore or separating the silver and lead. It is natural to assume that economic growth had something to do with the culture of the Athenians.

Similar association between an increase in the volume of production and wonderful artistic achievements are to be found in the Gothic Age in France and Italy, in the Renaissance of the late fifteenth and early sixteenth centuries in Italy and southern Germany, and in the Elizabethan and Jacobean periods in England from about 1580 to 1640. The first of these periods gave us Albertus Magnus, Thomas Aquinas, Roger Bacon, Giotto, Dante and the most majestic cathedrals. The second gave us

159

Michelangelo, Leonardo, Giorgione, Titian, Dürer and the architecture of humanism. The third gave us Shakespeare, Spenser, Donne, Milton, Hooker, Francis Bacon and the most delightful English music. Like the Athenian period in Greek history, each of these ages of giants was an age in which population grew and with it the command of men over matter in agriculture and industry. In the times of Aquinas, in the times of Michelangelo, in the times of Shakespeare, the merchant could look forward with confidence to a growth in his traffic from decade to decade and almost from year to year. During the reign of Saint Louis (1226-70), the production of silver and copper in Europe may well have increased threefold or more. During the lifetime of Leonardo (1452-1519), the output of iron in Styria, the leading center of the industry, grew at least fourfold. During the lifetime of Francis Bacon (1561-1626), the annual shipments of coal to London from the North of England mounted from less than ten to more than a hundred thousand tons.

A superficial historical observer might conclude that rapidly increasing industrial output is indispensable to great art, or even that it leads inevitably to great art. If he were a natural scientist, he might conclude that there is a symbiosis between a remarkable increase in the volume of material production and the development of a very rich culture.

Yet is there an inevitable connection between a rapid rate of growth in the volume of output and a more beautiful world? There are certainly examples from history which suggest there is not. It is hardly possible to show

Henri IV, Louis XIII and Louis XIV. If the test is conspicuous growth in measurable output there were for France only two periods of modest prosperity between 1560 and 1720, the first two decades of the seventeenth century (in literature the times of Malherbe and Urfé), and the sixties and seventies when Colbert directed the national economy. Both periods were followed by what students of economic growth today would regard as prolonged depressions, such as are no longer supposed to occur under industrialism. During these glorious times for French art, in the middle and later decades of the seventeenth century, France had some modest political successes and acquired some new territory. But few of the old or new French provinces were more productive, in point of volume, at the beginning of the eighteenth century than at the beginning of the seventeenth, or even the beginning of the sixteenth. After Colbert, the last three decades of Louis XIV's reign were times of much economic suffering. The output of several industrial products, such as coal and many varieties of cloth, seems actually to have declined. Vauban, the famous fortress-builder, the only general who, Voltaire tells us, preferred the welfare of the state to his own, has painted a picture of the material distress on the eve of Louis XIV's death. It is hardly less gloomy than the one painted by the Scotsman, John Law, who came forward with an offer to put things right by reorganizing the national finances and developing credit. Law was a special pleader who wanted to lay an accent on the distress of his adopted country in the interest of his reforms. So he might be expected to exaggerate. But the same reservation is hardly applicable to Vauban's description. Voltaire spoke of the long reign of Louis XIV, which lasted seventy-five years, as "an admirable century." What made it admirable was its art, the fine quality of its durable commodities, the style and elegance and growing moderation and reasonableness of an elite. The experience of French classicism suggests that national greatness can be independent of a rapidly mounting volume of output.

If a reduction in the labor costs of production and an increase in the volume of this world's goods were the measures by which to gauge a flowering in the arts, the sixty-five years from 1865 to 1929 in the United States should have been a finer period than any previously known to history. The population almost quadrupled. The railway, the automobile and finally the airplane spanned the country. Nearly all industrial work came to be done by machines. The output of manufactured goods increased about twenty-eight fold.[1] Scores of populous towns, many much larger than ancient Athens, were sprouting on a continent nearly a hundred times the area of Greece, with natural resources more than a hundred times as abundant. Judged by the material standards of the fifth century B.C., most of the inhabitants of these American towns were well off.[2] Judged by the less modest standards of modern America, there were in every

[1] Chester W. Wright, *Economic History of the United States* (New York, 1941), p. 707.

[2] But the differences in standards of living can be easily exaggerated. A recent comparison suggests that towards the end of the fourth century B.C., at about the time of Aristotle's death, the free wage earner in Athens could command about as large a quantity of the necessities of life as the British wage earner before the War of 1939-45 (Colin Clark, *The Conditions of Economic Progress* [London, 1940], pp. 164-67).

163

town a good many rich and a good many more about to become rich. The fancies of material abundance, published three and a half centuries ago by Francis Bacon in his *New Atlantis,* seemed on the point of being realized in dozens of communities. Young men full of enthusiasm and energy professed a desire in their off-hours from football, baseball or business to make culture hum. Millions of children were sent to school. Thousands of wives joined hundreds of clubs in the hope of exposing themselves to every variety of what has come to be called —not altogether happily—"intellectual" improvement. They sometimes embarrassed celebrated foreigners by asking whether it was proper to regard their town as "the modern Athens." If a rapidly expanding volume of output were the key to art and thought, the cultural drama of fifth-century Attica should have been repeated in a hundred cities. America should have added hundreds to the hundred greatest artists in the history of the world.

Yet, for all its wealth, this period in American history was not rich in artistic masterpieces; it was much poorer than the sixty years of Greek history from the Battle of Marathon to the Peloponnesian War. It was by no means as barren as some have supposed. An American cultural tradition was in process of formation.[*] But it has not been transmitted, like the French classical tradition of the seventeenth century, in customs and manners that became so instinctive that they are accepted without need of debate. During the period from 1865 to 1929 America was far from producing as many authentic

[*] Elinor Castle Nef, *In Search of the American Tradition*, New York, 1959.

164

artistic geniuses as appeared in France during what has been called "le grand siècle" from 1643 to 1715, a comparable stretch of measurable time. We may cite Whitman and Mark Twain and Henry James from these more recent years as all having literary genius, but their influence on American ways has been small compared with the influence of Racine, Pascal and Bossuet on French ways.* Henry James, like T. S. Eliot later on, put the United States behind him to become a British subject. A few striking and permanent, if scattered, works of literature appeared from other writers than Whitman, Mark Twain and Henry James. Among them the most perfect in artistry, perhaps, was young Stephen Crane's *The Red Badge of Courage*. A few brilliant imaginative artists lighted up the American scene—Sullivan and Frank Lloyd Wright in architecture. There were great historians—Francis Parkman and Henry Adams, a many-sided man of culture who fled the country almost as often as his fellow New Englander, Henry James. If Americans of taste and talent went abroad, it was partly because they found there a higher level of aesthetic judgment than they could discover in their own country, and so felt, incongruously and never fully, at home away from home.

During those times which are still recent, France gave the world the most beauty, above all in the art of painting. Americans found in France by far the greatest perfection in the visual arts. Paris and Provence became a sort of mecca for aspiring artists from America, Ger-

---

* Other American writers—Poe, Emerson, Melville—cannot be included because they were the products of an earlier period. (See V. L. Parrington, *Main Currents in American Thought* [New York, 1927] Vol. II.)

many, Spain, Russia, England, Italy, Holland and Belgium. Yet French population was stationary, and French economic growth slower between 1865 and 1929 than that of other Western nations.

What about those confections of sounds which create delight primarily through the ear? During the eighteenth century and at the beginning of the nineteenth, it was in Germany and Austria, the least progressive of the European countries on the industrial side—if industrial progress is measured by the multiplication of machines and the growth in volume of output—that the most wonderful flowering of music took place, with Bach, Gluck, Haydn, Mozart, Beethoven and Schubert. There and then lived the composers Schnabel chose to play. But the phenomenal growth of industrial output in the German countries came later. It came at the end of the nineteenth and the beginning of the twentieth century, and brought with it no music to compare with that of Brahms or Wagner, whose compositions themselves marked a decline from the musical delight of the late eighteenth and early nineteenth centuries.

An historical writer, the late Geoffrey Scott, has summed up the relationship between art and wealth in his illuminating book *The Architecture of Humanism.* "Prosperity is a condition of great achievements [in architecture];" Scott wrote, "it is not their cause. . . . Rich and flourishing societies have not seldom grown up, and are growing up in our time, without [making architectural history]. . . .* Scott's book is an essay in the

* Geoffrey Scott, *The Architecture of Humanism* (2d ed.: New York, 1924), p. 26.

166

history of taste, and these sentences of his can be applied aptly to all the arts. An increase in the command over nature possessed by any society is favorable to the creation of beauty, in so far as it frees men from working to provide for the bare necessities of life. Whether or not this freedom is used for purposes likely to lead to an age when beauty walks at the elbow of the citizen depends on the maintenance of a proper balance between the desires of the body and the needs of the mind and spirit. In so far as art is made to serve the material purposes which have been dominant in the triumph of industrial society, in so far as attempts are made to raise an art to a science, the works cease to be beautiful.

So historians who consider the history of art in relation to wealth are in a position to reach certain tentative conclusions which confirm those of one of the wisest of philosophers. "There seem to be two causes of the deterioration of the arts," Socrates tells Adeimantus in *The Republic*. "What are they?" he is asked. "Wealth," he says, "and poverty."*

It is not, therefore, by seeking first either riches or poverty that beauty is most likely to be achieved. The objectives of beauty and of mere economic growth are different, and the coming of industrialism has perhaps made this even truer than it was in the past. Just as we have to distinguish the purposes and values of art from those of science, so we have to distinguish them from those of economic growth, to the pursuit of which contemporary political authorities are coming to devote so much energy. It is possible for objectives of beauty and

* *The Republic* iv. 421 (Jowett trans.).

of material production to be in conflict, and such a conflict is perhaps especially likely to occur at a time when the search for quantity and speed has led men to undertake a different kind of work from that of the craftsman or the artist, whose purpose is to achieve a durable result however much time is required.

Here is an example from the crafts. I recently wanted to get some valuable art books repaired; their bindings had disintegrated, largely I fear through lack of care. Upon inquiry I found a woman in New York who did this work to perfection—the wife of a university professor. When she showed me the happy results, which had absorbed much of her skill and labor, she told me that hers was a dying craft. In all the eastern United States she was almost the only person with the knowledge and skill to practice it. She was disposed to try to remedy what seemed to her a danger that the craft might disappear. So she offered to give courses at a local university where her husband taught, in order to train at least a few young men and women in the work she loved. The university allowed her to offer one course, but no student enrolled. Students were apparently discouraged by the long apprenticeship which the craft requires. What is the use, they said to themselves, of restoring beautiful books at such a cost in labor? Better buy new, less perfect books that can be turned out quickly by machines. Anyhow, they felt, we are living in a world that changes so rapidly that it is out-of-date to seek the permanent, or to cultivate manual labor when so much can be manufactured automatically.

Whether the conflict between beauty and material

168

productivity is inevitable is another question. The possibilities of finding a refuge in the creation of beauty from the dangers that arise from the power unloosed by science and from the evil in man have hardly been explored. To explore them it will be necessary for men to want to redirect the economy towards quality. Is such a change compatible with the maintenance and spread of a decent material standard of living? Are the pursuit of beauty and the love of permanence, which is essential to it, enemies of economic growth? Such questions lead us to ask what history shows concerning the relations of art to wealth.

If poverty can be no less damaging to the artist than riches, does it follow that art contributes only to poverty? That would seem to be an illogical conclusion. It *is* necessary for the dedicated worker to choose between quality and quantity. The question is whether he can make the choice for quality—an exacting choice that requires all the thought and pains he can give—with a clear conscience that the effect of this devotion to the lasting things will not weaken the defenses of his country against obliteration by some foreign nation, that it will not add to the suffering of the miserable and the poor who are still so numerous especially in Africa, in the Near East and in Asia. What about that schoolteacher who became exasperated with the study of philosophy? Was she right in supposing it would be more human for us to distribute milk to the poor in a big city than to devote ourselves to beauty, to truth?

Each human being ought, of course, to give a personal answer. It would undoubtedly be awkward for society if every person took to the search for truth and beauty. But that danger seems remote! The question is whether in industrial societies a much greater importance can be attached to the arts and crafts, whether some can find the freedom to serve beauty entirely, without a lowering of the standard of living. Is there a place for wonder as part of industrialism, for wonder that relates not to outer space but to inner life where the happiness of men and women ultimately rests?

Towards the end of the nineteenth century, in the Anglo-Saxon countries, an extraordinary view came to be held that works of art are valueless economically—which is to say in so far as productivity is concerned. From the standpoint of the economist, wrote one of the fathers of economic history, Archdeacon William Cunningham, the Parthenon and other wonders of the great age of Greece were sheer waste. Athenian treasure, he remarked, "was locked up in forms that are artistically superb, but economically worthless."

These worthless forms have moved sensitive persons over twenty-five centuries of time and have always encouraged those who wanted to outdo themselves in their love of beauty. Cunningham seems to have had little sense of the utility of the useless. If poverty can harm the artist as much as riches, beauty in its perfection has always potentially a contribution to make to riches of every kind. In the sense that matters most, no one can be rich without it. Properly conceived and handled, beautiful things are a necessity for the good life of any individual. They help a person to surmount the hardships of life, just as they give him an incentive to be better than he is. A high standard of living in the fullest sense always depends on the independent search for higher standards of quality.

The success of European craftsmen and artists during the seventeenth and eighteenth centuries, especially in France and Holland, in fashioning beautiful furniture and musical instruments, beautiful tableware and all the embellishments for the luxurious and increasingly "civilized" life led in those times by a good many, had consequences that have been largely ignored by the scholars who have turned to history for instruction. It was not simply that these newly conceived commodities pleased an elite. Their beauty helped to arouse an admiration, that was new, for fine decorations and comforts to delight laymen in their daily lives. In Holland even humble farm houses often had paintings to decorate them. Such an incentive to the diffusion of charm and comforts, as developed in the seventeenth and eighteenth centuries, could never have been derived from the cruder domestic instruments of the Middle Ages, which were superseded by those of baroque craftsmanship. Almost all the craftsmen who fashioned these exquisite things had something of the joy that comes to the dedicated artist whose life is filled by creative work. They felt something of the value of what they were making. The beauty of these simple objects for elevating and giving fresh meaning and charm to homely, domestic needs —the need for food, for sleep, for warmth, for conversation and the exchange of confidences—set an example which had, in subtle ways, great utility. The fine quality of domestic surroundings aroused in widening circles

171

desires for similar goods in larger quantities. It was necessary to cultivate the taste of ever larger numbers of persons in order to get them to buy things that they needed to live above the level of their animal instincts, and so to provide markets for the manufacture of ever larger quantities of durable commodities.

At the outset industrialism seemed to offer means of satisfying qualitative as well as quantitative needs. The artistic side of this enormous economic effort has often disappeared in recent times in rush and hurry and in the craze for growth at all costs. But there is no reason to think that the need for delight has to be supplanted by a need for "guns and butter" and for noisy entertainment. A life cannot be well filled simply by abundance in sounds and pictures and speedy travel. Machines and automation will be insufficient in the long run to create a need even for more machines and automation. It is conceivable that, if left to themselves, mechanically manufactured products will glut the markets as did the wine and olive oil of the Roman Empire.

The idea of happiness, inspired by Chinese and Russian, by Persian and even African, as well as by both Greek and Christian experience, is founded on a combination of spiritual with material fulfillment. The indirect contribution which the search for beauty has made to modern and contemporary science and technology is immense. It is not always recognized because science is supposed to have evolved on its own. The triumph of science and modern technology offers existing societies the possibility of devoting to delight a more important part of human effort than was perhaps ever possible before.

172

The search for beauty would involve great changes, difficult to make, in the lives men are disposed to lead. It would involve also great changes in international relations, which great changes in the lives men lead alone could bring about. Such a consecration as is needed for beauty would be possible only if the proportion of the national budgets used for engines of destruction were greatly reduced. And that is possible only if a reasonable hope in peace, or at least in limited warfare, spreads.

Our *Search for Civilization* suggests on almost every page that in the long run a relatively peaceful world society is inconceivable unless there are fundamental changes for the better in human nature. So the great question is, can the cultivation of beauty contribute to such changes? Can it help to make better men and women?

Not by itself. It will perhaps be easier to convince men of the value of beauty than of the value of virtue. But without one we cannot have the other. The two are not alternatives. They complement one another. And with the world as men have made it in the late twentieth century there is no alternative to both, unless mankind is to revert to barbarism. Under existing conditions, in a world where some have gone almost mad for power and might, and where reason and cynical criticism, without love and constructive hope, can provide no paths to salvation, the great need is to put the most important—the useless—things first.

PART IV: VIRTUE

CHAPTER IX
Art and Virtue

BEAUTY CAN CONTRIBUTE to a peaceful world society only if it is the ally of virtue. Faith, beauty and virtue are all expressions of a combination of three supreme human attributes: integrity, taste and love. All are expressions of the inner life of the soul, of desires, hopes and experiences at depths which cannot be fruitfully probed by scientific research.

I have suggested that a work of art has an existence independent of its author. The nature of this influence depends not only on the work itself, but on those who read, listen to or contemplate it. In the case of a work which depends for its effects on being performed, the influence depends also on the persons who interpret it.

If, as has been suggested, the greatness of a work of art is revealed by richness and variety of meaning, it calls into play the deeper sides of human nature. It touches these in many situations and at many times in the lives of many different persons. To be beautiful, therefore, a work has to transcend the particular so completely as to be almost equally convincing and moving in different situations, in different countries and even in different ages. *Tom Jones* can again provide an example. Its style is peculiar to Fielding and to the times in which he lived, to an eighteenth-century world, with little steam, and no oil, electric or atomic power. Yet some of the statements and implications concerning life and love, of this most ingenious plot, are as fresh in the atomic era as they were when they were written two centuries ago. They are indeed in important ways—in forthright statement —more relevant to the life and love of some sensitive people of present times than the descriptions and implications of the best known novels published during the last thirty years.

When we speak of the richness and variety of meaning in a work of art and of its power to reach people fresh in many different places and times, we should not, of course, be taken to say that any interpretation a person allows himself to place on a passage in a book, a line in a poem, scenes in a painting or the rhythm and melody in a symphony, is legitimate. Richness is no excuse for license. While the spiritual and moral influence of a work of art is much less clear and predictable than the intellectual effect of a scientific statement, the very variety of meaning contained in the most beautiful creations of men and women sets limits to the interpretations, and these limits are no less rigorous than those set to the interpretation of a scientific statement when that is intended to mean only one thing. I have referred to Schnabel's playing of the greatest music composed for piano. It is true and revealing to say that no two performances by Schnabel were ever quite the same, and that each was a creative act because he seldom, if ever, misrepresented the spirit of a great work by his interpretation. Yet it is easy for a pianist or any interpreter to do just that. Comparisons between interpreters help to show how this is so. I heard Schnabel play one of the most beautiful piano concertos of Mozart—Kochel 467 —several times over in rehearsals and then in a concert. A few years after his death, I heard the same piece performed at Menton by another soloist of some reputation. That performance was a sharp disappointment. I know of no other music which is such a magical confection of exquisite sounds as Mozart's, and, perhaps for that reason, I know of none which can suffer more, or lose its tragic beauty so easily, in uninspired interpretation. On this occasion that happened.

This concerto of Mozart is certainly no less moving than any of the great Schubert quartets. Yet I heard one of these played two nights earlier in the same place— the one called "Death and the Maiden"—by an admirably understanding group of performers, and the Mozart concerto, in the spoiling which the soloist gave it, was made to seem less rich, less inspiring, than the Schubert quartet. No doubt Schnabel never played Kochel 467 as well as it could be played, but that night the pianist at Menton failed to perform it as well as it must be performed.

A poem differs from a concerto in that it can be read without an interpreter—or rather that one can be more

easily one's own interpreter as with a novel, an oil painting or a statue. But much of the finest poetry can be fully
appreciated only when it is heard, when it is beautifully
read or recited and acted. This is especially true of poetic
drama, of some plays of Shakespeare for instance, and
still more perhaps of every play of Racine. The public for
a play or a musical composition, unlike the public for a
work of visual art or a work of literature (unless that is
read in translation), is at two removes from the creator.
The listener at a performance of *Twelfth Night* or of this
Mozart concerto, Kochel 467, is interpreting, not the
work itself, as he does when he reads *Tom Jones* on quiet
evenings at home, but an interpretation of the work.

Once an artist releases a work the effects that it has,
the meaning it evokes, are in a measure beyond his control. Not that he is without responsibility for its influence. His responsibility is very great, almost infinitely
greater than that of any individual in his public, and
much greater than that of any interpreter. But he cannot
be held accountable, if he has created a masterpiece, for
either a misinterpretation or for the size of his audience.
These matters are outside his control, and, unless some
concern with them is a direct help to him in his art, it is
in the interest of his genius to put both of them out of
his mind.

While the artist is not responsible, beyond a certain
point, for the reception his work receives, it must meet
with comprehension and recognition if it is to survive, if
it is to have an influence on others besides himself. A
measure of success is indispensable for the artist, moreover, if he is to develop to the full his potential powers.
What is important is not that he should be in tune with

current values, for these may be almost valueless for art, it is that at least a tiny public should be in tune with beauty; that a few persons, with some confidence in themselves, should be able to recognize it and to respond to it when it is presented to them, to lift themselves, as the artist has done, beyond time, place and circumstance.

This relationship of the artist to the public is explained by Schnabel, in a small book that grew out of some observations he made on the occasion when he received an honorary doctor's degree from the University of Manchester.* The artist's inspiration is no more the creation of the public, than a man's voice on some high mountainside is the creation of the rocks, crags and peaks that rise about him. Yet the extent to which that inspiration is used depends, in a measure, like the use of the voice seeking an echo, upon the surroundings. If the echo comes, the mountaineer is encouraged to go on calling and to try out his voice in new ways. If he gets no response, he will relapse into silence. So it is with the artist. Even the greatest potential genius needs the nourishment that comes from recognition and understanding. They are as essential to a great painter as is water to the beauty of exquisite flowers. So the interpreter and the individuals who form a public have important parts to play in the future of art.

The fine interpreter must be an artist in his interpretations. As with the creator of beautiful objects, formal rules of technique have to be learned; they are indispensable, yet the interpreter must not be enslaved by

* Artur Schnabel, *Reflections on Music,* trans. César Saerchinger, Manchester, 1933.

them. In *La Vie de Marianne,* Marivaux remarks that it is necessary to "be better than one is in order to be great; if one is simply what one is one remains small." No interpreter can be better than he is if he depends on technique alone. Rules and forms are never enough for the beauty a man strives to interpret, any more than the geometrical mind, by itself, is adequate for dealing with any great problem of loving or living. As Pascal explained life is too varied and complicated for pure mathematical reasoning; its issues can be adequately met only by what he called the "nimbly discerning mind" (*l'esprit de finesse*). Of course the performer does well to know by heart the works he presents, provided memorizing them does nothing to narrow the freedom and range of inspiration necessary to the noblest and most stirring presentations. An inspiring interpretation is the result of personal discoveries; the great performer has to have time to make them. He has to make them for himself. Therefore the closer his spiritual kinship to the artist he interprets the better. It is only when his imagination and his heart are enlisted in the performance, and when they find a response among some individuals in the audience, who share the inspiration he evokes, that the work of the original artist is given fresh meaning.

Should a great interpreter explain his discoveries in words, as a literary critic does? Such an explanation can have value. But what is more important is that he should present the works in so meaningful a way that sensitive members of his audience make their own discoveries as he has made his.

Friendships, and the intimate, disinterested conversa-

179

tions which friendships facilitate, provide a further means by which artists and their interpreters can diffuse great discoveries. Nothing can take the place of the communion of creative conversations. Any notion that theories of art, arrived at scientifically, can enable human beings to decide correctly, according to rules, which works are great, which less great, and which not great at all, or that such theories can provide artists with the means of achieving masterpieces, is an illusion. The prevalence of such notions, of such inadequate substitutes for real criticism, has been facilitated by the new mass means of communication. These notions have put obstacles in the way of healthy judgment and of inspired vision. Such judgment and vision are essential if beauty is to provide a common language for civilization. They can be nourished only by that profound marvel in the beautiful which is behind every great artistic masterpiece that the world possesses.

These reflections show how important it is, both for the artists and for their public, that the processes of creative art and the experiences of the lover of art, should not be confused with scientific methods of verifying results. While the artist can sometimes learn from the new knowledge which science has provided, and from his relations with scientists, he must use all this material as an artist. Otherwise those complicated and moving experiences and problems that science cannot interpret or answer will be handled in inhuman ways. Attempts to deal with such experiences and problems creatively will be discouraged for want of an echo, at the very time when sensitive persons all over the world have an increasing need for the nourishment which beauty can provide.

It is by no means improbable that some works of art which, for the benefit of the race, should have endured, have never found an audience. There were too few influential people who recognized and cared about what the artist was doing to secure him a foothold among the public. The sea of noise, the nature of the assignments settled by those who control the policy of organs of publicity, the emphasis on current events and statistics of sales and circulation, to the exclusion of the deeper human issues likely to determine the course of current events, the plethora of cheaply composed books and pamphlets that floods the markets today, have certainly not made it any easier than it was before the triumph of industrialism, to detect the wheat among works of the mind, or to separate it from the chaff. In order to do this, in order to open to beauty and through beauty to life a fair prospect of its counting for good in the decades that are ahead, we must break away from two widely, if vaguely, held views concerning the future of art. The first is the notion that artistic effort and inspiration can merge to advantage with scientific effort and inspiration, that art can be properly interpreted and explained scientifically. Such a notion is related to the view that science and technology can be brought to devise ways of producing artists, much as they have made possible the multiplication of automobiles, and threaten to make possible the multiplication of robots. The second is the notion that the independence of the artist depends on his independence of ethical values, and that works of art, like

181

scientific theories, are neutral in their implications for virtue.

The notion that so-called scientific theories of art can help create artists is, in the main, an illusion. The prevalence of such *ersatz* criticism and approval, and its diffusion by the organs of publicity which are today successful in reaching many eyes and ears, interfere much more often than they help with the emergence in the lives of persons capable of sound judgments of visions of those ends of civilization fostered by a true and profound love of beauty.

By the richness and complexity which approach them to life and separate them from scientific statements, works of art cannot be explained to the advantage of either truth or delight by methods derived from procedures of scientific analysis. As with life, so with art: the "nimbly discerning mind" alone is capable of seizing something essential in the great artist's message. Pascal's very words about the nimbly discerning mind relate to the experiences of art as well as of life. ". . . The principles are familiar and open to general view . . . [But they] are so fine and so numerous that it is almost impossible that some do not escape us. Now, to omit one principle leads to error. . . ."*

Interpretation by the person who receives the work of art is an extremely delicate matter. Yet if such a person has a "nimbly discerning mind" and if his heart and imagination are enlisted by direct contact with the work, his experiences, along with those of others who share something of his discernment, offer the only sound basis

* H. F. Stewart, *Pascal's Pensées*, New York, 1950, p. 497.

for the verification of beauty. That is why Marcel Proust speaks of artistic verification as "la rencontre fortuite avec un grand esprit"*—the surprise meeting which a serious reader or observer or listener has with a book, a painting or a symphony, a meeting in which his assent is enlisted with abiding enthusiasm. There can be, in the sense in which the natural scientist uses the words, no objective test of this verification apart from the testimony of individuals. The very variety and richness of the work make it best that such an encounter with it as moves the sensitive person remains a personal discovery, which the discoverer shares and discusses fully with the persons who are closest to him in understanding and sensitivity. For the diffusion of these discoveries and the stimulus to the artist which they can provide, conversations with friends are the vital media. Nothing can take their place. Authentic individual delight of this kind by many persons establishes a work of art. It is the echo the true artist needs.

These reflections show how important it is, both for artists and their audiences, that the creative process and the joys of the meeting with its products, be kept independent of scientific methods of verification. However much an artist may gain in the materials at his disposal by concrete scientific knowledge and by conversations with scientists, it is always as an artist that he must order his materials and form his conceptions. Otherwise the complicated many-sided experiences and questions, which science can neither illuminate nor answer, the

* John Ruskin, *La Bible d'Amiens,* Paris, 1947, Préface de Marcel Proust, p. 92, n.

experiences and questions that are of such vital importance to the future of man, will continue to elude us. The
attempts by persons of great artistic talent and even
potentially of genius to handle them creatively will be
discouraged by the want of response, of echo, at a time
when the need of sensitive human beings for fresh delight is a compelling element in the search for civilization.

It has been frequently supposed across centuries of
time that art and virtue have little or nothing in common.
In the periods immediately preceding and following the
First World War, the public came to regard artistic colonies as hotbeds of moral laxity. Their view was not
entirely without foundation. A good many persons who
obtained temporary renown as artists did little by their
personal conduct or their work to prove that it was false.
In some quarters persons who aspired to become artists
felt that they were establishing their artistic reputation
almost as much through their irregular hours or their
prowess as drinkers, etc. as by the quality of the poetry
they wrote or the pictures they painted.[*] Gratuitous
acts, such as knocking down a headwaiter in a restaurant
for no reason or embarking on homosexual experiences
as a proof of independence, became models for the rising
generations of would-be artists.

What has not been recognized is that these activities
were no less irrelevant, and possibly even more harmful,
to the pursuit of artistic objectives than the confusion of
technique with beauty and the encroachment of science
upon thought. Such aberrations were an evidence of

[*] Cf. Malcolm Cowley, *Exile's Return* (New York, 1934).

184

the growing materialism which was bound to damage art by submerging it among values with which it has little or nothing in common.

In so far as moral philosophy can help to teach the artist just proportions in the conduct of life, in so far as it can help him to acquire good habits, it is bound to help him as an artist. It will enable him to put his body at the service of his mind and spirit; not to make his mind and spirit the slaves of his body. True inspiration, as Plato suggests in some of his Dialogues, is a divine madness. It is not the madness produced by worldly drunkenness.

The artist can be inspired to the intensity of conviction woefully lacking in some recent art only by a consuming love of beauty, justice and truth. If the existence of absolute values is denied, as it has come to be so largely in recent times, then a great source of artistic inspiration is removed. No one can look at the wonderful scenes carved on medieval abbeys, churches and cathedrals without realizing that the craftsmen who created them had a compelling sense of the difference between right and wrong conduct, and that they could count on the audience who came to worship to share their "prejudices," as modern social scientists might call them. The craftsmen had a compelling sense of the difference between justice and injustice, as these were conceived in the mind, with the help of faith, and not as they were laid down arbitrarily by a despotic ruler in order to increase his own power. In a more recent age, what gives such strength to the works of Balzac or Dostoevski is the deep sense of moral values felt by their authors, combined with the detachment with which as men of letters

185

they were able to write. The standards of right and wrong are essentially the same in two writers of such completely different temperament and background as Balzac and Trollope. Their work is equally dependent upon the existence of these standards. It is of little or no significance that Balzac's personal habits as a writer were irregular and excessive, while Trollope's were a model of methodical balance annoying to persons who take for granted that beauty can thrive only on eccentricity of conduct. Balzac and Trollope were united in this:—both were concerned in portraying, in different ways, the overwhelming value of goodness and the overwhelming iniquity of evil.

The responsibility of the artist is of a different order from that of the scientist. It is an integral part of the work that he does. The meaning of a scientist's results for those who understand them can hardly be equivocal. But the consequences of these results, when they are utilized for practical ends, can be dangerous to the future of the human race. And the only way open to the scientist of meeting the danger of destruction inherent in some of his results is to suppress them, to conceal them from the world.*

The consequences of artistic achievements are very different. As we have suggested, the variety and richness of works of art make the nature of their effects up to a point equivocal in the highly complex realm of experience which it is the glory of the artist to explore. So the direct spiritual and moral influence is much less clear and predictable than the intellectual effect of a scientific

* See above, pp. 103-04.

186

statement on those who understand it. A work whose ethical *intentions* are above reproach, even the Bible, can be used by a weak person as a justification for doing evil; a publication whose ethical intentions are vicious, for example a piece of pornographic writing or a magazine filled with erotic photographs, can sometimes fortify the virtue of a strong person.

The risks have to be taken. Beauty is an explosive compound. But the dangers from its explosions are small in comparison with those in the explosions made possible by scientific progress. And the refuge from these dangers offered by delight, combined with virtue and faith which nourish our inner lives, has hardly begun to be recognized. Art touches those strains in the individual which enable him in rare cases to make himself over, to set an example for those who are about him, and when he occupies a position of power, to lead with unexpected compassion and justice. Science can equip men with new knowledge which is of *practical* use, but the *wise* and *humane* use of this knowledge depends on the existence of better individuals. Science cannot produce them. The resources for making them rest with beauty allied with faith in man's potential capacities to serve the good.

What folly, then, it would be to suggest that the search for beauty be absorbed by science. That would be a way of abandoning the hopes which the search for beauty can arouse, on the ground perhaps that the greatest works of art have sometimes corrupted men or women who were already on the slope leading to the abyss. The admonition to man in the Christian Gospel reminds us of the artist's true responsibility. It is to rise above himself, both as an artist and a man, for if art and life gain by being drawn together, every split between art and the good is at the expense of both. If the future of art would be jeopardized by merging it with science, its future would be strengthened by its alliance with virtue.

CHAPTER X

Virtue and Civilization

FAITH IN A JUST and loving God is a gift independent of and superior to wealth. The strengthening and the spread of faith as a civilizing force is bound to take time. The existing resources for its propagation—churches and clergy as at present organized and inspired—are inadequate. There is only a small minority of persons on this planet who now deeply believe that man is linked to eternity. And among this minority very very few alas are moved by the words of the Gospel: "Thy will be done, on earth as it is in heaven." Most rare are those who care profoundly whether or not they bring their lives, in a spirit of humility and self-criticism, into greater accord with this message.

Moreover it is not only among a few Christians that hopes are nourished for a true civilization such as has never existed. Non-Christians too yearn for a better, a more virtuous future for the human being. Some of them judge the beautiful and the good according to human standards, without believing that there is such a thing as absolute Truth, that there is a superhuman Being, Who

189

is beyond time, Who was here in the beginning and Who will remain after all the worlds of which we can have knowledge are gone. Others share the Christian's faith in absolute truth and in a supreme being. The Christians who yearn for a better temporal world need these persons' help and support. They need the Christians' help and support. Are not they all children of God? The pure in heart (with their faults and blemishes, their sins and doubts) are not sufficiently numerous to afford the loss of a single one. The Christian should leave the non-Christian free to find his own way. Is it not equally desirable that the non-Christian leave the Christian free to find his? They should unite in the joy of seeking, in the most diverse ways, essentially similar values. Believers and nonbelievers, who have hope in man, have too much in common to part company over the religious differences that seem to divide them, now that the future, and even the existence, of our race depends on their common efforts to live for more enduring ideals than violence and war.

Towards the end of the sixteenth century, when the Christian faith was a matter of much more concern to men generally than it is now, the great English theologian Richard Hooker wrote: "While riches be a thing which every man wisheth, no man of judgment esteems it better to be rich than to be wise, virtuous and religious." His words suggest that even so profound a believer regarded wisdom and virtue as objects separate and distinct from religion, though complementary to it.

No wise theologian has ever claimed that faith and revealed knowledge, by themselves, are adequate to meet all the problems of society and of the individuals who compose it. No wise theologian has claimed that faith makes reason, observation and experiment unnecessary, when we are concerned with the realities of the temporal world. The nature of virtue, the conditions that are likely to make it a less scarce commodity than it has always been, were within the province of classical moral philosophy. It is now more urgent than ever before to break the chains that prevent persons everywhere from being their best selves; which means being better than they seem to others, or even, in the case of the profoundly humble, better than they seem to themselves.

The traditional objective of philosophy has been happiness—happiness of the individual, of the state as a collection of individuals, and of humanity. Like so many words today, "happiness" has for most of us no precise, commonly accepted meaning. Many Americans seem to identify it with what is frequently called "having fun." That is an overworked phrase, lacking precise meaning. "Having fun" refers mainly to filling one's life with absorbing activities, preferably of a lighter nature, and usually in nonworking hours, though there are some for whom work is "fun," indeed the principal "fun." The phrase evokes the idea of being engaged in something, it seldom matters what, to the point of forgetting one's troubles.

Obviously such an objective, by itself, has no necessary connection with permanent values. It has seldom anything fundamental to do with the overcoming of pride, wherein is found the true loss of self in the deepest love.

Everyone, we are told, has his own way of having a good time. "One man's meat is another man's poison" is a well-worn sally that applies to any activity regarded as absorbing which advertisers seek to exploit. So "having fun" leaves us without any hierarchy of joys independent of individual caprice. Such fulfillment as it offers is mainly synthetic.

Happiness had a different meaning for the great philosophers of antiquity. For them it was not a matter of individual whim. As the wisest among them saw it, happiness consists, not in seeking pleasure for its own sake, but in gaining it from doing the right things or behaving in the right way, according to the accumulated wisdom of the race. Happiness depends upon the establishment in the individual and in society of the most perfect harmony possible between the needs of the body, the spirit and the intelligence, with reason and its more humble companion, common sense, the masters over both body and spirit. Plato and Aristotle were in essential agreement over this theoretical idea of happiness. But happiness can no longer remain a theory; it must either become a partial reality or be wiped out altogether. The ideal state would be one in which the needs of all the citizens for material comfort and security from violence are satisfied in the ways most compatible with the happiness of the citizens, and with a noble life in this Platonic and Aristotelian sense.

Such a concept takes for granted the existence of certain absolute values; it takes for granted the existence of good moral, intellectual and artistic habits. In Aristotle's *Ethics* the existence of good habits does not depend upon the establishment of fixed rules of conduct that will fit every situation. There are certain actions—murder, theft and adultery—which Aristotle regarded as wrong altogether. He would presumably have regarded the "happiness" which is obtained from committing such acts as counterfeit. This was because he believed that a permanent moral code exists for all men and all societies independent of our sensations. According to that code, whose values are not scientifically demonstrable, there are certain things that a human being should never do. Therefore men should strive to make their inclinations, their desires, conform to this code. But, for Aristotle, moral virtue generally consists in the most appropriate response to a given situation, in the action that is most perfectly in accord with wisdom under the circumstances. Circumstances differ. They are obviously not the same now as in Aristotle's time.

The nature of men's legitimate desires is continually changing. In Elizabethan England, for example, almost everyone seems to have consumed alcoholic beverages in quantities that are now confined to a small minority of the population. A passage in *Othello* suggests Elizabethans thought the drinking powers of Englishmen exceeded those of foreigners. Iago shouts: "Some wine, ho!" and sings a drinking song. " 'Fore Heaven, an excellent song," says Cassio, his lieutenant. "I learn'd it in England, where (indeed) they are most potent in potting; your Dane, your German, and your swag-belli'd Hollander . . . are nothing to your English . . . he drinks you, with facility your Dane dead drunk; he sweats not to overthrow your Almain; he gives your Hollander a vomit ere the next pottle can be fill'd."

The statistics with which we moderns are deluged,

show that this was no idle boast. At the end of the seven-teenth century Gregory King, one of the early statisti-cians, estimated that in England almost a sixth of the national income was spent on alcoholic drink in various forms, as compared with about a ninth in France and about a tenth in Holland. The expenditure per head on drink in England was about twice as great as in France and much greater than in Holland.[1] The beer and ale consumed per capita was at least four times what it is in modern England; perhaps twenty times or more what it is in the United States.

When Shakespeare put those lines in Iago's mouth, the real income of the English worker was probably somewhat less than in King's day, almost a hundred years afterwards. But the per capita consumption of light alcoholic drink was probably greater.[2] The Elizabethans were not only capable of wonderful feats in drinking bouts; beer came to form, after bread, the chief element in the diet of the common man. He consumed as much with a meal as many an American ordinarily does in a month.

From the point of view of learning there are, broadly speaking, two possible attitudes towards changing wants.

[1] Gregory King, *Natural and Political Observations and Conclusions upon the State and Condition of England* (1696) (bound with George Chalmers, *Estimate of the Comparative Strength of Great Britain* [London, 1804]), pp. 47, 64-65, 67. Cf. Colin Clark, *National Income and Outlay* (London, 1937), p. xvii; *The Conditions of Economic Progress* (London, 1940), p. 89.

[2] J. U. Nef, "Industrial Growth in France and England, 1540-1640," *Journal of Political Economy*, XLIV, No. 5 (1936), 647-48; "Prices and Industrial Capitalism in France and England, 1540-1640," *Economic History Review*, VII, No. 2 (1937), 165, 168-69, 172-73.

It is possible to treat them as phenomena worthy of investigations designed to establish the facts. An historian, a sociologist or an anthropologist, for example, may collect data on the wants of different peoples at the same or different periods of history. He may compare them as a matter of scientific curiosity. He may discuss the effect of indulging them, in so far as the physical and the biological sciences seem to warrant him in drawing conclusions. If, for example, it can be shown that constant heavy drinking and incessant cigarette smoking shorten the average length of life, it follows that men in a society where drink is used as a food or tobacco as an hourly companion will have a shorter life-expectancy, *if other things are equal,*° than men in a society where there is little smoking and where beer or wine are drunk only in modest quantities. Such facts are published and often obtain wide publicity. They sometimes cause alarm. It is for others to evaluate their meaning. But where are these others to be found in a world in which everything that cannot be proved scientifically is treated as chiefly fantasy, without general application? Any judgment concerning the aesthetic or ethical or even the social value of different wants for the individual or for society lies outside the province of the learned man.

This is a possible way for a learned man to regard men's desires. It prevails in practically all the universities of the contemporary world in so far as research and teaching are concerned, whatever moral interpretations are put on these findings privately by some professors.

What other possible point of view concerning chang-

° See above, pp. 5-6.

ing wants could a learned man adopt? He might attempt to discover what is good for man and for mankind— aesthetically and ethically even more than intellectually. Having reason and compassion, justice and love as guides, he could set about examining concrete cases with the object of suggesting tentatively what wants and what combinations of wants, contribute most to the happiness of the individual, the nation and humanity. That would be one way of indicating possible roads to civilization. If tentative conclusions could be reasonably drawn, they might help provide substance in a search for firm ethical values. They might help, in this way, to make an emphasis on such values the heart both of elementary and high school education, and a part of intimate family life. If the future of beauty depends on its association with virtue, this second attitude concerning desires is far more important than the first.

It could provide a basis for a new development of moral philosophy, at a time when the invasion of humanistic and social studies by scientific methods has led to the denial that ethics, in the traditional sense, can be a science.* Like religion, moral philosophy is nothing when it ceases to be concerned with permanent values. A fresh outlook on changing wants offers a new hope that happiness need not be left entirely to chance.

In referring as I have to elementary and secondary education and family life, I am not thinking of rules, or of rewards and punishments, though these have a place in the family and the school. I am thinking of the inquiries that learned men should carry on and the oppor-

* See above, p. 70.

tunity they would have for expounding the results of these inquiries, in ways that could help children, young people and also mature men and women, who teach and raise families, to make choices based on permanent moral values. If it were possible for wise men to agree, within certain limits, on the order of goods in a world where people and commodities abound as never before, they could light lanterns to help those persons in all countries who want to seek the good in their professions. They might help to guide artists and churchmen in making their choices on a plane which transcends their particular time and place. That, in turn, might create common bonds between peoples of all races and nations and religions. By indicating, even imperfectly, the directions in which the good is to be found, by giving flesh to the ideal, as the moral philosopher should strive to do, he can help men to find within themselves ways of lifting their lives onto a nobler plane. A great man, such a statesman and writer for instance as General de Gaulle, is first and foremost his own creation. But there would be a greater chance of finding others worthy of the ideal, if young and old alike were nourished in the courage of being honest, and if it were more and more recognized that the search for virtue is the key to the search for civilization.

The lack of any inspired guidance in the realm of morality is one of the characteristic features of our age. In the Western countries persons are much less aware of firm principles than were their ancestors in the eighteenth and nineteenth centuries. It is true that everywhere in the world today states have their laws, institutions, their rules; that everywhere there are established ways of educating the youth, established ways of choosing leaders, ways that are often somewhat lacking in the finer shades of ethics. These laws and rules and ways differ considerably, not only as between societies and countries, but as between groups, between churches. What is almost entirely lacking are principles which transcend these most divers laws and rules and habits—principles capable of placing justice and understanding above all laws and rules and ways, so that laws and rules and ways can be changed for the better, can be more generously interpreted, modified and softened, when that is possible, or strengthened, when that is necessary.

In view of the decrease in deep aesthetic and moral experiences which has accompanied the triumph of industrialism, fewer persons have a genuine and decided ethical preference one way or another today than a century or more ago. With the decrease in the direct experience most people have with the processes by which the commodities they eat and use are grown and made, they have often little basis for judging even underlying material values which go beyond quantity. So they seek advice. There is no lack of "experts" to supply them with it on special subjects, though a man does not always find the perfect agreement that would be reassuring if he takes the trouble to consult more than one expert. These experts are full of information in terms of facts and figures on their special subjects, but to understand the individual case requires much more than expert knowledge.

No man, no matter how strong and wise he feels himself to be, is prepared to act on every issue that confronts him without advice or guidance. Where are we to seek personal guidance when it comes to a choice involving matters of morality, social justice, wisdom or beauty? The natural place to turn is to a priest or pastor, if one belongs to a church, or to a professor or teacher, or to one's father or mother, brother or sister, intimate friend or godparent. Yet most of these persons, not excepting the pastor and even the priest, have been trained in the modern doctrine (if it can be properly so called) that there is nothing approaching firm standards behind conduct. Disagreement on philosophical issues is now frequently regarded as beneficial to society. This is not the disagreement of rational discussion, it is not even the emotional disagreement which can be reconciled by affection and forgiving. (Both those disagreements can be constructive, leading, as they alone do, to more comprehensive generalizations, and to deeper more durable understanding and love.) What we have rather than this is disagreement for the sake of disagreement, disagreement for the sake of the ego. Everyone is then left free, from the standpoint of morality, to say and do almost anything he likes, provided he doesn't break the law and get caught, with a completely free conscience and often with an almost completely empty mind.

The lack of any firm judgments which people respect in matters of beauty and ethics is not surprising when we remember that moral philosophy in the Platonic or Aristotelian sense—the field of ethical values—has been almost entirely abandoned. We go to doctors and surgeons to find out how to keep well. We go to investment counselors to find out how to invest our money. We go to interior decorators to find out how to furnish our flats.

199

When the advice we obtain from the three experts creates a serious moral or spiritual issue, as it often does, we have only our own opinion to fall back upon. It rarely occurs to us that books written by wise men of the past might help us. When it does, we realize that we have wasted our lives without reading them. We live in an age when indexes and other short cuts (useful as guides to information) are wrongly regarded as substitutes for culture. We have experts in every field except the supremely important one which encompasses all the others. In that alone the decisions are left to private urges and eccentricities.

It is a mistake, nevertheless, to assume that the individual's predilections—his "own philosophy" as he is fond of calling them—are in fact determined without outside influences. We all receive advice without knowing it. In matters of morality, intelligence and aesthetics, pressure is brought to bear on us from the time we are born. It is brought to bear on us by the mores of our schoolfellows and playmates, by the very lack of judgment concerning great ethical problems which we generally find in our parents and our friends, our teachers and the ministers in the churches we visit, if we happen to go to any. More interested pressure comes, as we grow older, from advertisers and from the businessmen they represent. These persons are eager to enlist us as consumers and, less frequently, as workers. Politicians seek our votes—and sometimes when we ourselves are dependent on political office—settle for us, and against our judgment, what ways to vote. The very fact that no one has referred us in early life to principles, or led us to saturate ourselves with books where they can be found, enables almost any clever person to give advice and to gain influence concerning current issues. Such advice is full of philosophical implications. In a society which recognizes no special competence except in the limited cases susceptible to scientific proof, such advice masquerades frequently as knowledge. Men use it "to make friends and influence people" on matters of morality, social justice and aesthetics, not always with the best motives and almost never with the best thought.

Moral and even intellectual and aesthetic issues are often placed at the mercy of anyone who finds it advantageous to direct them for purposes of business, politics or graft. In the universities the learned man, if he is also a good man, because of his very modesty is made to regard any "prejudice" he may have in favor of impersonal and durable standards as a private matter, if not an idiosyncrasy. He may be allowed to try to guide his own life by these "prejudices," but if he speaks of them in public or adjusts his learned activities to them, his efforts are dismissed as "evangelical." His example is treated as irrelevant to learning. A pastor tells him that he ought not speak on behalf of goodness unless he joins the pastor's church. If he joins it he must leave matters of justice to his pastor, who has usually ceased to have any firm judgments concerning them. If he happens to mention his "prejudices" to his colleagues and suggests that others might find it in them to want to share them, he is told that he takes life too seriously.

Is it better for man to have matters of art and morality settled exclusively by the give-and-take of the market place and by the improvised daily relations between men and women—sometimes moral, sometimes amoral and at least occasionally immoral—or is it better to have a few gifted men who devote their whole lives to these questions, who are passionately seeking to benefit mankind, with no hope of private gain beyond a competent salary, exercise an influence in the realm of ethics? Some of those who take the first view have been saying that time will repair all the evils which seem to flow from it. They are like the people in a pacifistically minded country who hope and say that time will take its enemies off its hands. Time is neutral. Unless wise men grasp its opportunities and work for good, evil will gain the day. On the whole, time worked in favor of decency and justice in nineteenth-century America and Europe. This was largely because Christian ethics influenced men to try to make it work that way. Now that standards have broken down, is there not danger that bad money will drive out good? In the natural sciences we rightly take it for granted that special gifts, training and study, together with special enthusiasm for the subject, confer on a man a special competence. Is it only on behalf of welfare generally, on behalf of the virtuous life, that the scholar is to be discouraged from feeling enthusiasm? Is it only on behalf of justice and of love that those few individuals on whom a gift for wise judgment is bestowed are to be discouraged from setting an example? Is it only in the department of happiness that the universities are to hang up a sign, "To Let"?

The very fact that needs change shows that the great philosophical questions of the relative moral, intellectual and aesthetic value of different kinds of needs, judged in terms of happiness, are a part of experience. This shows that moral philosophy should not be divorced from life, and that a new outlook on wants could provide a means of giving them a meaning in terms of life such as they have never had before. The aim of moral philosophy would then be to guide wants in directions that contribute to happiness. In the ideally ordered society of the future, which we seek, all branches of learning would be allied with moral philosophy in this aim.

If it becomes possible, with the help of a new attitude towards changing wants, for wise men to agree to some extent on the order of goods in a world full of riches and people as never before (and alas at the same time full of misery), then they might help, without coercion of any kind, to guide men and women intelligently and disinterestedly in the direction of their better selves. They might help men and women to cultivate the best life offers them for the sake of those they love, for ultimately it is only in serving others that one serves oneself. By indicating in concrete terms, however imperfectly, the nature of the ideal, as the moral philosopher should try to do, in communion with the small disinterested groups which we seek to form, he might help individuals everywhere to fall less short of leading good lives.

We need to look at the matter of guidance in terms of its effects on the lives led all over the world because of the growing ascendancy of industrialism. As a result of the achievements of science and technology, lives are led in different ways, farther from the soil, farther from nature, than they were ever in the past. Is it more desirable for the future of our race, that virtue should be adapted, should be adjusted, to industrialism and to the institutions and habits, the prejudices, the ways of life, that have grown up with industrialism and to a large and increasing extent because of it, or that these institutions and habits, these prejudices and ways of life should be adapted, should be adjusted, to virtue? For me at least the answer can hardly be in doubt. If the human beings of our time and of the future bow and submit to the circumstances that are created by the rise of industrialism and by the "misplaced concreteness" of university research, if they adapt themselves and the societies to which they belong to the laws, the rules, and to the dogmatic prejudices embodied in these rules and laws, instead of reforming the laws and rules and interpreting them in the light of justice, mercy and love, they will remain at best much as they are. They will contribute nothing to a search for civilization. At the worst people will lose, as the two World Wars suggest they have been losing, the advance in the domains of conduct—the decency and the tender manners—without which industrialism itself could not have spread with anything like such speed during the nineteenth and twentieth centuries. At the worst they will return to what Guizot called "the barbarous indifference for the lives and deaths of their fellow men and women . . . which Christianity alone succeeded in rooting out of human societies."[*]

In the domain of virtue the old ways of behaving inherited from the Christian ethics, which once pre-

[*] *Histoire de France,* vol. i (1872), p. 415.

204

vailed as an ideal, have grown increasingly rusty and
ineffective because we have taken them for granted instead of renewing them and giving them new meaning
by relating them to the changes of the industrialized
world. All I know of history leads me to disabuse those
who suppose that virtue can take care of itself. Com-
placency is a great weakness which threatens, at worst,
to destroy the race, and, at best, to compromise the life
of man. If men and women everywhere are to meet the
challenge which confronts them in the late twentieth
century, they cannot allow their moral strength and the
wisps of gentleness and love that they feel for others, to
diminish. More than ever before we have need of the
tenderness, the humility and the love which Christianity
at its best nourished, by witnessing their eternal validity.
Virtue and love need as never before to penetrate the
search for delight; they need to penetrate religious worship. It is the purpose of those groups of friends that we
are trying to form to help this to happen. It seems to me
that the only way of putting science, technology, commerce and business at the service of man, is to render
virtue and love the supreme guides in all human activities.

How can this be done? The widely held view that
ethics is not a science in the sense that chemistry or
physics is a science is a sound one, though I have the impression that John Dewey held that it could be made
into something approaching a science, and that his notion of how this might be done could be reconciled with
the objectives of small groups of dedicated servants of
wisdom. The attempt to make ethics into a science, like

chemistry or physics or even biology, can end only by confusing it with logic or psychology or some other branch of knowledge more closely related to the natural sciences. Should it not be an art at least as much as a science, the art of seeking the good? While the results of scientific, psychological and anthropological research can be useful to the new moral philosophy, philosophical inquiries themselves cannot be conducted primarily under the direction of methods appropriate to the study of the natural sciences. Ethics cannot be partial, as any particular science must be, any more than it can be indifferent to problems of good and evil. It can never take anything for granted. It can never say, as other disciplines so easily can, "other things being equal." In reaching their results, moral philosophers must strive to take into account all aspects of matter, space and time, and of human beings as individuals, as members of an institution, of a community, of a nation, of a church and of the world.

Notwithstanding all the fine words that have been written about it, philosophy has always suffered, even before the advent of modern science, from being too solemn and even sanctimonious. The philosopher appears too frequently with a wry face. The divorce he is inclined to accept between his philosophy and his life— and which is caricatured so uproariously by Fielding's Square when Tom Jones catches that philosopher in bed with Molly Seagrim—is healthy for neither the philosopher nor for philosophy. A lack of naturalness in his philosophy helps make a fool of him in his life. Philosophy, for all its long words, and in spite of the justified view frequently taken of it as the most difficult and learned of subjects, deals with matters that are of daily concern to all sensitive human beings. Ethics, in particular, ought to deal with those matters which Schrödinger tells us the scientist cuts out of his picture, those which are close "to our hearts." A philosopher without a heart is hardly a person fitted for this assignment.

When I first studied philosophy it was with a professor of the pragmatist school at the University of Chicago who had come to Harvard for a term to replace a colleague absent on leave. I had known him well and recognized him as a human being. But it was difficult to find much that was human in his lectures. This was partly the fault of the philosophers he talked about. In his account of Descartes I remember the stress he laid, quite properly no doubt, on the sentence: "I think, therefore I am." There is so little in these cold words to give warmth to a person who cares deeply about the small things of life, and isn't it the persons who care for those things, out of which the big things are made, whom philosophy should have for its public? I remember getting much more helpful guidance at the time from two middle-aged ladies neither of whom had been to college or had ever taken a course in philosophy.

I recently talked with a foreigner on this subject. He had once professed philosophy abroad and had later acquired, by direct observation, knowledge of the professorial life led in American universities. He told me that he had discovered in the United States some encouraging signs of philosophical creativity, which, if

207

nourished, might lead in the direction of the harmony and the unity we seek everywhere. That promise did not come from the philosophy departments or from persons trained in philosophy. He found it rather in the ideas and sense of mission of some isolated professors, researching and teaching in other departments, and in the asides which a rather larger number of younger professors made in their off-hours from work. He found it too beyond the doors of these American institutes, with their laboratories, their workshops, their classrooms, their lecture halls, libraries, chapels and offices.

What is needed is homely genius for bringing the deepest experiences of life into the orbit of art. This genius, which can never reach even the tentatively exact and final conclusions that scientific genius can, offers the listener or the reader the opportunity to draw inferences for himself on the basis of wisdom. A "philosopher" of the kind that is needed would not make the mistake of insisting too much, of trying to prove his argument logically when it is beyond logic, of rubbing the lessons in. He would not make the mistake of identifying a universal ethics with any nation or with any religious sect. Direct preaching almost never wins persons who are worth winning—who have the power to move mountains. They can be won only by helping them to win themselves. So the philosopher who is a preacher, like the teacher whose only resource is violence (as these two are portrayed by Square and Thwackum in *Tom Jones*), deadens the spirit of free inquiry both in himself and in his charges. Behind the philosopher's genius there needs to be a long and disciplined training in the thought and culture of the race, and perhaps even more important, in the discipline of personal suffering surmounted through charity and compassion which alone can clothe creative thought and art with the highest moral intention. The small groups of which I have spoken can become centers for such training and for the disinterested discussions which are necessary for the formation of a higher, more universal level of opinion in the domain of ethics.

It is not for the philosopher, as a philosopher, to take a position on controversial and transitory issues, or to interfere with the private affairs of individuals. The philosopher has the task of trying to formulate and develop principles in relation to concrete events and changing institutions. No doubt it is valuable and desirable to try, in so far as this is possible, to predict what is likely to happen in the future. But a science of prediction is vulnerable because there is always that strange creature—man—whose hopes and inspirations are in many ways the same, in many ways invariable. His influence is nevertheless unpredictable because of the great range which prevails within this invariable—the human person—and both women and men at their best (as well as alas at their worst) are almost certain to upset the predictions of social or "behavioral" scientists. Three decades ago the most reputable demographers confidently predicted that in Europe and North America the last years of the twentieth century would be marked by a crisis of depopulation. Now, with equal confidence, and on the basis of the same kinds of evidence, they predict instead a crisis of overpopulation. The possibilities of human nature are as inexhaustible as the race itself, and so the subject man presents as a living being is as complicated as the problems of prediction are simple—or rather, we should say, have to be rendered artificially simple if answers have to be given.

It is the human being, and not the material conditions he may meet twenty years hence, which should be the first concern of those who seek for truth. It is not beyond their powers to help shape the future in defiance of prediction. It is, therefore, for those who create with philosophical intent to kindle the best in others, and, by helping them to be themselves in excelling themselves, to provide examples independent of every particular interest and every specialty. It is the purpose of the groups devoted to the search for wisdom to represent the eternal hope which God implanted in man, to husband His divine gift to us in the concrete earthly world to which, for better or worse, we are all committed.

Complete happiness is beyond the possibilities offered by the temporal world in which we all live. Paradise will not be found in outer space or on the moon any more than here. It can only be beyond matter, space and time. But it is not the best way to move towards paradise, to serve the Kingdom of God, to mitigate the purgatory which this world so often imposes on the most honest and decent and gifted, it is not the best way to lighten the lot of human beings, to renounce hope that, by efforts based on the individual's free will, the world for the first time in history can provide a happier home for men and women striving to achieve the good for which Christ was crucified. The search for perfection in all domains of temporal life can hardly be indifferent to God. The road leading towards perfection is the only road to civilization.

210